THE ELEMENTS OF FENG SHUI

Man-Ho Kwok is the foremost Feng Shui master working in Europe today. He studied for twenty years before qualifying, and is now in considerable demand as a consultant on Feng Shui to the Chinese business communities in London, Manchester and other major cities. He became well known after he was called in to help with the design of London's docklands. Man-Ho Kwok is now becoming known as a consultant outside the Chinese communities as Westerners catch on to the fact that his methods really do work.

Joanne O'Brien is a well known authority on Chinese religion and philosophy, and is the author of a number of popular books on Chinese matters including *The Contemporary I Ching*, *Chinese Myths and Legends* and *Lines of Destiny* (Chinese face and hand divination).

The *Elements Of* is a series designed to present high quality introductions to a broad range of essential subjects.

The books are commissioned specifically from experts in their fields. They provide readable and often unique views of the various topics covered, and are therefore of interest both to those who have some knowledge of the subject, as well as those who are approaching it for the first time.

Many of these concise yet comprehensive books have practical suggestions and exercises which allow personal experiences as well as theoretical understanding, and offer a valuable source of information on many important themes.

In the same series

THE ELEMENTS OF
FENG SHUI

Man-Ho Kwok
with
Joanne O'Brien

ELEMENT
Shaftesbury, Dorset ● Rockport, Massachusetts
Brisbane, Queensland

© Man-Ho Kwok and Joanne O'Brien 1991

Published in Great Britain in 1991 by
Element Books Limited
Longmead, Shaftesbury, Dorset

Published in the USA in 1991 by
Element, Inc.
42 Broadway, Rockport, MA 01966

Published in Australia by
Element Books Limited for
Jacaranda Wiley Limited
33 Park Road, Milton, Brisbane 4064

Reprinted 1992
Reprinted 1993
Reprinted February and July 1994

Cover design byMax Fairbrother
Typeset by Selectmove Ltd, London
Printed and bound in Great Britain by
Biddles Ltd, Guildford & King's Lynn

British Library Cataloguing in Publication Data
O'Brien, Joanne 1959-
The elements of feng shui
1. Geomancy
I. Title   II. Man-Ho Kwok
133.333

Library of Congress Data available

ISBN 1–85230–220–8

CONTENTS

Acknowledgements

With thanks for their help and support to Elizabeth Breuilly,
Kerry Brown, Jo Edwards and Martin Palmer.

INTRODUCTION

Why is it that some places emit a sense of well-being and peace and others a feeling of unease? How can it be explained that some families or businesses seem dogged by bad fortune and others blessed by success? A feng shui master would not hesitate in his reply – the forces at work in the land and in the cosmos may be in harmony at one place and in chaos at another. If the orientation of a building clashes with the contours of the land, the flow of a river or the direction of a road, if the position of a front door or a piece of furniture blocks the flow of ch'i, the life-giving energy, it is usually a matter of course that misfortune will follow.

Feng shui is not a matter of luck and is more than a system of omens. In the west it is considered a bad omen to walk under a ladder and there is little that can be done about it; in the east it is bad luck to have a tree planted directly outside the front door but something can be done to counteract its effects. Instead of being passive recipients of fate those who believe in feng shui can actively shape it. In the words of Stephen Feuchtwang:

The truth of the matter is that omens tell only of the workings of fortune itself, and the Chinese have, of course, their share

1

of such omens too, while feng shui purports to be a way of manipulating luck. What is especially interesting about feng shui is that it is very much more like a system of beliefs, supported by expert practitioners of feng shui who have at their disposal a vast literature and the tools of their practice.[1]

For the Chinese feng shui has traditionally been a way of life. It is both an art and a science that has influenced the shape of Chinese cities, palaces, villages and cemeteries. It is a force alive in the environment and as long as we follow its flow, which is also the flow of the universe, the Tao, we can achieve the three great blessings; health, happiness and prosperity. Furthermore, extreme steps are not usually required to achieve this harmony. A well-positioned door, tree or aquarium filled with goldfish may be enough to improve your fortunes.

Feng shui literally means 'wind and water'. These are the elemental forces which shape a landscape and also have the hidden power to affect human fortune. They are at work everywhere and in many forms, particularly in the flow of ch'i and in the balance of yin and yang. Ch'i is continually on the move, condensing, evaporating, inhaling and exhaling. If it is blocked by the position of a door of a building it can cause disaster but, by contrast, it can also evaporate in a space that is too open. Yin and yang are opposing forces in a continual state of flux and tension. They represent female and male, light and dark, water and fire; they are in everything that exists and changes. Since the feng shui expert is familiar with the flow of ch'i and the balance of yin and yang across the landscape and through buildings or cemeteries he can advise on planning or identify the source of bad luck in an existing building.

Knowledge of feng shui is not, however, the prerogative of the feng shui master. Although he has a more detailed knowledge of the mysterious workings of the universe through Chinese arts and sciences, there are practical principles which anyone can follow. Many involve common sense, others are learnt, and others involve intuition (see chapters 5–8). For example, a house on low-lying ground is likely to be flooded during heavy rains or a tree planted too close to the house is likely to affect the foundations. This is bad feng shui. At other times the view from a building may be pleasing to the eye and provide a sense of well-being. That in itself is positive feng shui.

Feng shui is often referred to as geomancy, more popularly known in the west as 'earth magic', but feng shui in fact embraces more than western geomancy. It is not only part of everyday life, catering for physical comforts, for mental well-being and financial security but also harnesses far greater cosmic forces that it is believed affect the universe. Through the use of the compass the feng shui expert aligns human activity with these forces (see chapter 3). Feng shui is now becoming increasingly popular in the west as a development of traditional western geomantic practices and is considered to add a more sympathetic dimension to the relationship between people, structures and their environment. While most people outside the Chinese community would find it strange to pay for the services of a feng shui expert as well as a surveyor before buying a house, it is not unusual for businesses in the United Kingdom and elsewhere to pay for such a survey.

The outward signs of feng shui are still most obvious in Hong Kong and Chinese communities throughout the world. Many Chinese hang a ba-gua, a small mirror surrounded by lines known as hexagrams, outside restaurants, homes or offices. Its purpose is to deflect bad fortune that may be caused by the position of the front door or the direction of the road facing the building. Sometimes the mirror alone is not powerful enough to deflect bad fortune and wind chimes are also hung in the doorway since ghosts and spirits fear their sound.

If the mirror or chimes are not sufficient to resolve bad feng shui, structural alteration may be necessary and many businesses or families are willing to carry the cost of expensive alterations. Even before a building is constructed in Hong Kong a feng shui expert is naturally part of the design team. When the Hong Kong and Shanghai Bank was built it was the tallest building in the area, a sign of authority; it was facing north, a favourable direction for this site; it had the protection of the hill known as the 'Peak' behind and the good fortune to be on a slight gradient that led down to the wide, open space of the harbour. Meanwhile, the Bank of China was building a new bank nearby and had delayed the construction until work on the Hong Kong and Shanghai Bank was completed. To assert their authority over the financial transactions of Hong Kong, their building had been built slightly higher than the Hong Kong and Shanghai Bank. The feng shui of the neighbouring buildings also deteriorated since it was believed that the sharp corners of the Bank of China were like daggers slicing their businesses and the reflective windows turned bad fortune back on to its neighbours. To avert further bad luck and to protect clients and staff, the managing directors of neighbouring office blocks hung ba-gua mirrors or small tridents on the outside wall of their office to stave off the effect of the sharp corners. A third office block, to be called Central Plaza, is currently being built on Hong Kong island. When it is finished it is intended to be the tallest building in the area, at least another floor higher than the Bank of China, and will symbolically have financial dominance over surrounding businesses.

Once you are familiar with the basic rules of practical feng shui, there may be no need to call in an expert. He or she would say that if you believe in the power of feng shui and know where to look you could not only reverse your misfortune, but also improve your mental and physical well-being. For many the power of feng shui is a matter of life and death and they believe that careful planning could possibly avert tragedy.

When Man-Ho Kwok, (the co-author of this book) lived in Hong Kong, he knew of a married couple who had lived happily for more than fifty years in their farmhouse in the New Territories. They had raised three sons and two daughters. Their daughters had married and gone to live with their in-laws; two sons had also married and brought their wives to live in the farmhouse. Between them the sons had three grandchildren, and when a third son was due to marry the parents realised they couldn't offer the new couple their own bedroom. Determined to keep the family under one roof, they arranged for an extension to be built to the right-hand side of the house. The extension was completed within a month and immediately after their marriage the youngest son and his new wife moved in. Three months after their marriage the youngest son was electrocuted when he was trying to fix an old electric fan. Three months later, the second son died in a road accident and a fortnight later his mother fell seriously ill. She was rushed to hospital but it appeared that Heaven could not help them and she died on the journey. The father could not believe that in the space of a year he should lose three of his family and griefstricken he turned to his friends and neighbours for help. Although the feng shui of the house had been assessed before it was built, the neighbours suggested a feng shui master should visit once again to identify the source of this misfortune.

When the feng shui master arrived he drew out his compass and carefully checked the main door, and every room in the house. The positioning of the rooms and furniture was perfect and the master was puzzled. He checked the back of the house where the pigs and poultry were kept and once again the reading appeared to be excellent, even the hill behind the house protected the family not only from the bad weather but also from misfortune. He moved to the front of the house where he came across the extension and then he knew why the family had suffered such tragedy.

'Knock this extension down immediately', he ordered. 'This is the source of your unhappiness. The spirit of the

5

White Tiger resides at the right-hand side of your house and the spirit of the Green Dragon on the left. Since you have built the extension the Tiger has become so powerful that the Green Dragon can no longer control it. The Tiger is now free to roam your house and to consume those who live there.'

The feng shui master pointed out to the family that this structural imbalance would always bring misfortune. They may have had better luck had they consulted the almanac before choosing a day to start the construction or they could have hung powerful charms. The situation would even have improved had they built the extension on the left-hand side of the house, the side of the Green Dragon. He could only suggest that they demolish the extension.

Not all structural mistakes have such severe consequences as the example above, and can usually be resolved without resorting to demolition or extensive rebuilding. According to feng shui principles, fortunes can be improved by rearranging furniture, changing the internal decor or by small structural alterations in the home or office.

On a recent visit to Hong Kong, Kwok Man Ho was invited to lunch by a friend who ran a clothing factory. During the course of the meal, the man admitted that his business was in decline and that if trade continued like this he would be bankrupt within the year. He knew his factory was well-sited and for years his business had been flourishing, but since moving to a new apartment his luck had changed. Kwok Man Ho agreed to visit his friends and after choosing an auspicious day for a feng shui reading from the Chinese alamanac, he arranged the visit. Kwok Man Ho was led into the living room but even before he had a chance to take the feng shui compass out of its case he spotted the source of his friend's financial problems. A door had been built linking the living room to the dining room at a position in the room known as the wealthy point. The good fortune that should have accumulated at this point was disappearing through the doorway and into the dining room. The ch'i or life-giving energy was dispersing in too many directions. Kwok Man Ho then assessed every room in the house using his compass and the feng shui proved to be perfect. The following day the door was filled in and a new one built further down the wall. Three months later he was invited to a celebratory dinner by his friend who informed him that business had never been better.

In an ideal world everyone could choose the perfect site to build a house or to site a grave, but for the majority means and circumstance dictate the site. The geomancer[†] can suggest ways to alleviate the misfortune associated with the site but cannot guarantee health, good luck and prosperity for the family. Some may be resigned to their fate and accept bad luck as a consequence of feng shui but the geomancer will not accept such fatalism. It is said that a true and honest heart can overcome the misfortune associated with the most inauspicious of sites. Abiding by the guidelines of feng shui is an aid to a successful life, but the most influential factor is personal conduct. We are born within a certain framework and are subject to parameters that are beyond our power to control, but a great deal of what we make of life lies in our own hands, which is why the Tao and the arts and sciences are there to guide us. The Chinese believe that if we can operate within the way of the universe then good fortune will follow. The following story illustrates this belief:

Many centuries ago there was a feng shui master who was known for his skill but who was also easily moved to anger. One hot summer he was commissioned to assess a burial site in the mountains far from his home. It had taken him three days to walk to the site and a day to carry out his work. After sleeping in a small mountain shelter, he had packed

---

[†] Although the brief of the feng shui expert is wider than that of the geomancer in the west, he is referred to in the practical sections of the book as a geomancer. The feng shui expert is also referred to as 'he' since it is traditionally a male profession.

his compass and papers and set off for the long journey home. On the second day, he had run out of water in the overbearing heat, but as he surveyed the fields of rice ready for harvest that lay across the plain before him, there was no sign of a well.

In the distance, he saw a woman and three children working in the fields and so he headed in their direction. The woman stopped winnowing the long stalks of rice and her three sons lay down their scythes and baskets to stare at the stranger.

'Can I ask you for a bowl of water. I am exhausted and thirsty', said the feng shui master, 'I cannot walk any longer unless I have water'.

The woman crossed to a nearby tree and bent down to uncork the pitcher of water that stood there. She poured clean, cold water into a wooden bowl, but before she handed it to the feng shui master she threw a small handful of chaff onto the surface of the water.

The feng shui master immediately felt anger welling up inside him and grabbed the bowl from the woman without a word of thanks. As he sipped the water, he continually had to blow the chaff to one side. He was convinced that the woman had insulted him, and as he quietly emptied the bowl of water he thought of his revenge.

'Do you live here?' asked the feng shui master.

'Yes, I live with my three sons in the hut at the far end of this field. My husband died two years ago and I have three sons to care for and feed. As you can see we are poor people.'

The feng shui master slowly gazed towards the hut and at the surrounding land. 'No wonder you have such bad fortune', he replied. 'I can tell you now that the feng shui of your house is unlucky. As long as you stay here you will only know misfortune, but I think I can help you. Beyond the other side of that mountain there is a plot of land and a dilapidated house and although the land needs clearing and the house repairing, the feng shui is excellent. I suggest that you move there as soon as possible.'

The woman and her sons bowed down to the feng shui master in gratitude, and without reply he raised his bags over his shoulder and left them. In revenge for the chaff thrown on his bowl of water he had directed them to 'Five Ghosts Dead

Place', a site so inauspicious that the sons would be lucky to reach the age of twenty.

Five years passed before the feng shui master returned to the area to see how the family had fared. As he approached the house the mother came out to greet him and bowed before him.

'Do you remember me?' he asked.

'Of course I do. How could I forget your kindness. We followed your wise advice and you can see how my lands are fruitful. Two of my sons are studying for government jobs, my third son will soon be leaving to study with a wise teacher. Please come into my house and accept a meal.'

As the feng shui master sat eating the rice and vegetables offered by the woman he looked around in amazement at the newly plastered walls and the new furniture.

'How can this be?' he thought to himself, 'the site hasn't changed, there is still bad feng shui and she has no charms to protect herself'. 'I don't understand what has happened here', he admitted to the woman, 'I sent you to a site that had such bad feng shui you couldn't possibly have survived here and yet your family is flourishing. What have you done that Heaven can bless you in this way?'

'Why did you decide to punish me when I am innocent? What have I ever done to hurt you?' asked the woman in surprise.

'When I needed water, you gave me water but instead of clean water you threw a handful of chaff on the surface to spite me.'

'Didn't you realise?' laughed the woman, 'it was a hot day, you had travelled a long way, and I knew you were exhausted. You were so thirsty that you would have swallowed the water in one go and the shock of the cold water would have been too much for you. You had to blow on the water to clear the chaff each time you took a mouthful and so you drank it more slowly. I was trying to protect you.'

The feng shui master nodded his head in recognition.

'Now I understand. I sent you to an evil place but your action has been rewarded. Every day Heaven and the Buddha will bless you.'

9

1 · LIVING IN HARMONY

In Chinese philosophy, yin and yang are the two cosmic forces that shape and balance all life. They are opposites in a continual state of flux and tension, and through this dynamic they produce life. Yin, which is feminine, luminous and fluid, is present in the moon, rain and floods. It is counterbalanced against yang which is masculine, heavy and solid, the force that is in the sun, the stars and the earth. The forces of yin are in the ascendency as the cold and damp of winter approach and are on the wane in the warmth and new growth of the early spring as yang asserts itself. Yin and yang are never represented as gods nor are they associated with divine power, they are purely natural forces that were brought into being through the emptiness that existed at the beginning of time. Their creation and activity are described in the Huai Nan Tzu (circa 120 BCE), a study of natural philosophy recorded in twenty-one volumes:

> Before heaven and earth had taken form all was vague and amorphous. Therefore it was called the Great Beginning. The Great Beginning produced emptiness and emptiness

11

Yin/yang symbol

produced the universe. The universe produced material forces which had limits. That which was clear and light drifted up to become heaven, while that which was heavy and turgid solidified to become earth. It was very easy for the pure, fine material to come together but extremely difficult for the heavy, turgid material to solidify. Therefore heaven was completed first and earth assumed shape afterwards. The combined essences of heaven and earth became yin and yang, the concentrated essences of the yin and yang became the four seasons, and the scattered essences of the four seasons became the myriad creatures of the world. After a long time, the hot forces of the accumulated yang produced fire and the essence of the fire force became the sun; the cold force of accumulated yin became water and the essence of the water force became the moon. The essence of the excess force of the sun and moon became the stars and planets. Heaven received the sun, moon and stars while earth received water and soil.[1]

Feng shui is the way of divining yin and yang in the landscape. Feng shui literally means wind/water and is the art and science of reading a landscape so that the buildings for the living and dead can be sited where the balance of yin and yang is positive and where ch'i, the life breath, can circulate freely.

Feng shui is founded on the belief that the hills and rivers have been and still are eroded by the forces of wind and water. The term *feng shui* represents the power of natural environment which is alive with hidden forces.

By observing the patterns of change and understanding the natural processes of the land, a feng shui expert can discern favourable directions and good or malign influences at any spot on the ground. Experienced in Chinese calendrical and natural philosophy, the expert can assess the landscape and recognise an imbalance in the forces of yin and yang, identify constructive or destructive movements between the five elements, or identify a blockage on ch'i, the life-giving force.

These notions are all central to the practice of feng shui but an expert will also give a detailed reading for a given site by consulting his compass. Each ring of the compass dial is inscribed with symbols which are a physical representation of the cosmos with its array of interrelated real and imaginary forces, phenomena and creatures.

Feng shui is a way of living harmoniously with, rather than conquering, the natural world. It is a model for dealing with reality, a means of positively aligning the fortunes of an individual or community with the Tao – the inevitable, powerful and harmonious way of the universe.

Feng shui dates back at least three thousand years, although the philosophies and symbols it incorporates date back to an earlier period. The earliest reference to feng shui commentaries exists in the *History of the Former Han Dynasty*, with reference to the *Golden Box of Geomancy* and *Terrestrial Conformations for Palaces and Houses*. Neither book has survived. The two books that were to have formative influence on the feng shui masters, and which are also included in the Imperial Encyclopedia under the same titles, are *The Burial Classics* by Kuo P'o (fourth century CE) and the *Yellow Emperor's Dwelling Classic* by Wang Wei (fifth century CE). The latter book distinguishes between yin dwellings for the dead and yang dwellings for the living. This titular division still exists, and through the centuries far more manuals have been written as a guide to the siting of tombs and cemeteries as opposed to palaces, offices and houses. There was much speculation and theorising on burial sites since a well-sited grave would not only appease the spirits of the dead, but also bestow good fortune upon their descendants whose well-being depended, to a large extent, upon appropriate burial and the continued care of their ancestors. The feng shui manuals that focus upon sites for the living are preoccupied with the immediate concerns and practicalities of everyday life.

Although feng shui may have been frowned on through the centuries by the sophisticated and practical Confucians, it was an essential part of Chinese existence, and most people at some time in their lives would have consulted a geomancer. A geomancer was traditionally referred to as feng shui *hsien-sheng*. Hsien-sheng is a title of respect, although the words cannot be directly translated. Geomancers were treated with deference and frequently carried to and from the site in a sedan chair. They were employed on a part or full-time basis and traditionally received hospitality and gifts as opposed to fees. Besides being honoured for their literacy geomancers were believed to possess insight into the mysterious workings of nature and an understanding of powerful cosmic forces beyond the scope of the average citizen. They considered themselves scientists, and information on geomancy appears in the Imperial Encyclopedia under arts and divination, not under religion.

When a geomancer was present at a funeral he was there as a guide, familiar with the powers that shape this world. He prepared the practical ground for a priest who then stepped in to act as the intermediary between the land of the living and the land of the dead. The geomancer may only have been a consultant in this process but he was often held in awe and suspicion because of the power he wielded. His decisions could affect the fortunes of a family and so it was dangerous to ignore his advice but at the same time it was difficult to prove incompetence if the family suffered bad luck in the years to follow. Nevertheless, the family would once more call in a geomancer to assess the site and hopefully suggest a way to dispel the misfortune. There is a story told not only of the geomancers' questionable status but also of the secret forces they could summon up:

> In a place north of Ch'ao ch'ing in Kuangtung province there is the Seven Star Peak and to its west is a hill that closely resembles the back of a turtle whose head is formed by several large stones jutting out into the water. A rich man had summoned a geomancer who advised him that ten years ago the turtle opened its mouth and this unusual event was due to happen again on a certain day that year. He advised the wealthy man to bury the bones of one of his ancestors there. And so the rich man took the coffin of one of his ancestors, placed it into a boat and, accompanied by the geomancer, they sailed to the site of the turtle rock. As they approached the whirlpool that lay close to the head of the turtle, the geomancer waited until the whirlpool gave a particularly loud roar and then ordered the rich man to push the coffin into the water. The rich man did as he was told, but no sooner had he disposed of the coffin than he began to regret his actions. He had failed in his duties to his ancestor by disposing of the body in an unorthodox place. He accused the geomancer of trickery and deceit and took his case to a local magistrate. After hearing the evidence, the geomancer was ordered to return the coffin to the rich man. The geomancer asked the magistrate to lend him his sword and returned to the stone turtle. He climbed onto the turtle back and with a swipe of his sword he sliced off the stone head and, by doing so, destroyed its power. The coffin resurfaced and the geomancer returned it to the rich man. When the rich man opened the coffin, he immediately regretted his decision – the body of his ancestor had become covered in golden scales.[2]

The geomancer could also prove to be divisive in family life. His decrees on the siting of a tomb could create family squabbles or litigation and this unfilial conduct could in its turn disturb the harmony that should govern a burial. At times, the geomancer was a threat to the state itself. Ch'ing emperors are said to have taken precautions against families who the geomancer predicted would form a new dynasty.

The geomancers' judgement no longer wields the same power over ruling families or governments although his pronouncements are not taken lightly and his knowledge is still widely respected. As in the past, there are those for whom feng shui is a full-time occupation and although they use the same tools of the profession, they are more likely to turn up for a consultation in a three-piece suit than a traditional gown.

Although feng shui is no longer officially practised on mainland China it is an effective part of life in Hong Kong and the New Territories as well as the many Chinese communities worldwide. Even without consulting a geomancer, Chinese settlements and tombs still follow the ground rules of feng shui. The dead should be buried on a south facing slope, above the town and protected from malign spirits by mountains to the north. The good fortune resulting from the protection of the ancestors flows down the slope and into the town which, facing south, receives the benign influence of the summer sun. The city of Canton in southern China is a good example of this planning, and most Chinese towns will try to incorporate these basic elements as much for practical reasons as cultural ones.

2 · SYMBOLS OF HEAVEN AND EARTH

Feng shui divines the forces that are in heaven and on earth so that humanity can live in balance with them. Heaven, earth and humanity share a mutual responsibility to maintain the harmony of the universe. Humans fulfil their role by understanding the cosmological forces of creation and by knowing how to be at one with their flow and change. The basic principles used to identify these forces in feng shui are the same as those that govern Chinese arts and sciences such as astrology, physiognomy and acupuncture. The most important principles are listed below.

THE FIVE ELEMENTS

The five elements are types of energy that are effective in all substances and changes. Although they are given the names and qualities of natural phenomena they were probably devised to explain a concept in the same way that yin and yang are the names given to explain the dynamics of life. The elements are one of the ways in which Chinese philosophy relates to the growth and decay of the universe. According to Needham:

> The conception of the elements was not so much one of a series of five sorts of fundamental matter ... as of five sorts of fundamental processes. Chinese thought here characteristically avoided substance and clung to relation.[1]

The five elements are arranged in a highly systematised set of relationships whose origin cannot easily be traced. In the *Shu Ching* or Book of History, Heaven decreed the order of the universe in the 'Great Plan with its nine divisions'. The first of these divisions is the Five Elements:

> Of the five elements, the first is named water; the second, fire; the third, wood; the fourth, metal; and the fifth, earth. (The nature of) water is to soak and descend; of fire, to blaze and ascend; of wood, to be crooked and to be straight; of metal, to obey and to change; while the virtue of earth is seen in seed-sowing and ingathering. That which soaks and descends becomes salt; that which blazes and ascends becomes bitter; that which is crooked and straight becomes sour; that which obeys and changes becomes arid; and from seed-sowing and ingathering comes sweetness.[2]

In any individual substance or phenomenon all elements are present in greater or lesser proportions. As is indicated in the 'Great Plan' they have the power to create or destroy each other, thus giving rise to a new element. Their interaction is also an indication of the good or bad fortune that may befall a person or place. This is the order in which they produce or destroy:

wood produces fire	wood destroys earth
fire produces earth	earth destroys water
earth produces metal	water destroys fire
metal produces water	fire destroys metal
water produces wood	metal destroys wood

The five elements are the link that gives symbolic expression to the heavenly stems, earthly branches and the twenty-four points of the compass, the astrological terms that mark out the divisions of time and space. Not only are the five elements a common reference for astrological observations and definitions, they are also a system to correlate everything in the universe which can be grouped into fives, often on an arbitrary basis. The table below illustrates some of these correlations.

	Wood	Fire	Earth	Metal	Water
Planet	Jupiter	Mars	Saturn	Venus	Mercury
Colour	Green	Red	Yellow	White	Black
Taste	Sour	Bitter	Sweet	Acrid	Salt
Five classes of animals	Scaly (fish)	Feathered (birds)	Naked (human)	Hairy (mammals)	Shell-covered (invertebrates)
Yin and Yang	Lesser yang	Greater yang	Equal balance	Lesser yin	Greater yin

The elements are also reflected in the shapes of hills and mountains and in the direction of watercourses. The main forms are illustrated on page 20.

When watercourses meet or combine the elemental rule of production or destruction is applied, for example,

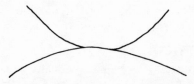

One fire or two woods entering a metal wall would indicate that the family will endure misfortune for many generations. Depending on the interpretation of the watercourse fire destroys metal or metal destroys wood.

19

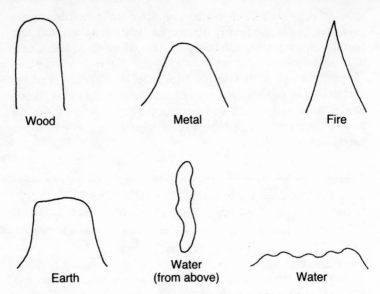

Elemental shapes in mountains, hills and boulders

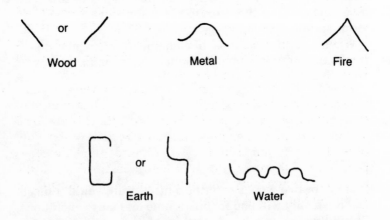

Elemental shapes in water courses

20

In the illustration below water enters metal and since metal produces water the family can expect prosperity and honour for many generations to come.

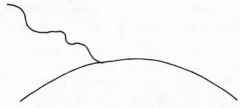

Although not referred to directly on every ring of the compass, the geomancer can correlate the elements with each ring in the same way that they can be correlated to phenomena in the universe.

THE HEXAGRAMS

Through the creative interaction of yin and yang the universe is in a constant state of change. But this change is not haphazard – it is part of an overall pattern, ordained by Heaven, that is the Tao or the way of the universe. By following the Tao and accepting the changing patterns, not only of the seasons but of personal fortune, we maintain harmony with Heaven and earth. If we fight change, we upset the balance between Heaven, humans and earth and by doing so we are going against the Tao.

At the moment of creation, all things are given a specific nature by a principle called li. Li is order and it is expressed through the Tao. The order of every living thing is ordained at the moment of coming into being and it is the duty of all things to abide by li through correct and righteous behaviour. The importance of order is summed up in the following commentary from the Ch'un Ch'iu – Records or Annals of Spring and Autumn:

'Allow me to ask,' said Chien Tzu, 'what we are to understand by ceremonies (li)'. The reply was, 'I have heard our late

21

great officer Tzu Ch'an say, "Ceremonies are founded in the regular procedure of Heaven, the right phenomena of earth, and the actions of men"'. Heaven and earth have their regular ways, and men take these for their pattern, imitating the brilliant bodies of Heaven and according with the natural diversities of the earth. Heaven and earth produce the six atmospheric conditions, and make use of the five material elements. These conditions and elements become the five tastes, are manifested in the five colours, and are displayed in the five notes. When these are in excess they ensure obscurity and confusion, and the people lose their proper nature. The rules of ceremony were therefore framed to support that nature.[3]

The essential resonance within the universe and the unceasing pattern of change within an ordered framework is reflected in the eight trigrams and their sixty-four possible combinations. Each trigram is made up of three lines. The lines can be broken (- -) or unbroken (—). The broken lines are yin and the unbroken lines are yang. The eight trigrams reflect the gradual movement from absolute yin to absolute yang and back to absolute yin again in a never-ending cycle. When the trigrams are placed into pairs they form sixty-four combinations or hexagrams. The hexagrams and commentaries on each are recorded in the I Ching – the Book of Changes. A hexagram is chosen through the random selection of coins, positioning of sticks and historically through the appearance of cracks in a tortoise shell as a result of heating. It is by allowing random choice to govern the choice of hexagram that an individual is able to tap into the flow of the universe and be guided by the inevitable flow of the Tao.

The I Ching probably dates back beyond the Chou dynasty and is the product of an ancient system of oral divination. The commentaries and appendices that accompany the hexagrams were concluded by the Han dynasty. Tradition has it that the original hexagrams, known as the Former Heaven sequence were formulated by Fu Hsi, the mythical bearer of the gifts of civilisation. He is credited with the invention of the Chinese calendar and the civil administrative system amongst other things, but he is best remembered as the bringer of the eight trigrams. One legend tells how he first saw the eight trigrams marked out on the shell of a turtle and it is known also from investigations at a Chou dynasty site that turtle shells inscribed with crude characters or signs were used for divination. In turtle or tortoise shell divination a small hole was made in the shell and heat applied until the shell cracked, and the lines which subsequently formed were then read by someone skilled in the art of divination. It is likely that these cracks were the inspiration for trigrams since shells have been found inscribed with lines, often three in number. There is no indication of how or when the trigrams developed into hexagrams but by the early Chou dynasty the sixty-four hexagrams were in existence.

The Former Heaven Sequence

In this sequence line one, the innermost line, determines the trigram's cosmic force and sex, and the second line determines the extent of yin or yang, male or female, and if the balance is still the same, then the third line is taken into account. For example, judging from the first line, Ch'ien, Tui, Li and Chen are yang and male; the remaining four are yin and female. Judging from the second line, Li is more male and yang than Chen since it has two unbroken yang lines compared to Chen's two broken yin lines. The sequence itself represents the gradual accumulation of yin as it travels up the trigram to form absolute yin and then its decrease to allow for the accumulation of yang to form absolute yang and then the growth of yin again in each trigram.

The Former Heaven sequence represents the annual cycle of yin and yang as they wax and wane through the seasons and enables the geomancer to relate to the forces of the cosmic yin and yang.

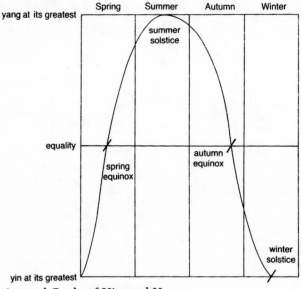

The Annual Cycle of Yin and Yang

The Later Heaven sequence is attributed to King Wen (circa 1160 BCE). A story tells how he was captured by invading forces of the Shang dynasty and imprisoned for a year. During that time he wrote short and cryptic descriptions for each hexagram. Many of his judgements consist of a few characters without pronouns or tenses. These judgements were elaborated on by his son, King Tan, who produced equally cryptic commentaries which are open to interpretation according to the diviner.

The Later Heaven Sequence

This sequence does not reflect the seasonal cycle of events but does reflect the points of the feng shui compass. The trigrams show the balance of yin and yang at a particular spot on the ground. This reading is then compared with a reading from the Former Heaven sequence so that the cosmic yin and yang can be balanced with the localised yin and yang. By doing so the greater invisible forces of Heaven can be compared to the visible features on the land.

The commentaries and interpretations that accompany the hexagrams in the I Ching are not always relevant to the compass reading and are often used simply to inform the

*Trigram Associations and Correlations for the
Later Heaven Sequence*

Hexagram (Later sequence)	Name and attribute	Family relationship
Ch'ien	creative strong	father NW
K'un	receptive yielding	mother SW
Chen	arousing movement	eldest son E
Sun	gentleness penetration	eldest daughter SE
K'an	danger flowing water	middle son N
Li	adherence dependence	middle daughter S
Ken	steadiness stillness	youngest son NE
Tui	joy serenity	youngest daughter W

Hexagram	Natural phenomenon
Ch'ien	heaven
K'un	earth
Chen	thunder
Sun	wind
K'an	moon
Li	sun, lightning
Ken	mountain
Tui	lake

geomancer of patterns of change. The trigrams are important for direction, determining yin and yang balance, for their associations with symbols on the compass and for their correlation with anything else that can be formed into an eightfold group.

THE SIXTY-YEAR CYCLE

The Chinese calendar revolves around a cycle of sixty years. The cycle is formed by the interaction of the Ten Heavenly Stems and the Twelve Earthly Branches which are units of time and place. Each year, a stem is paired with a branch and a new combination is produced so that the Heavenly Stems are repeated five times in this calendar and the Earthly Branches are repeated six times. In the first year the Heavenly Stem is Chia and the Earthly Branch is Tzu, following the yearly rotation this combination will take sixty years to appear again.

The branches, in particular, give information about time and place, although they are the means by which the heavenly bodies can express their influence. On the feng shui compass the branches mark directions of the earth, and identify the ch'i of the earth, the dragon ch'i. The stems are associated with water and can be used to mark twists, turns and branches of watercourses.

When they stand on their own, the Earthly Branches correlate to the twelve animals of the Chinese horoscope, twelve months, twelve double-hours of the day, twelve directions, and twelve groups of animals associated with the twenty-eight constellations. The twelve animals of the Chinese horoscope do not correspond to stars or groups of stars as do the twelve animals of the Western zodiac.

Legend tells how the Jade Emperor invited the animals of the earth to a banquet, only twelve animals arrived at the palace and each was allocated a year and an hour of the day for their efforts.

Heavenly Stem	Earthly Branch
Chia	Tzu
Yi	Ch'ou
Ping	Yin
Ting	Mao
Wu	Ch'en
Chi	Szu
Keng	Wu
Hsin	Wei
Jen	Shen
Kuei	Yu

Heavenly Stem	Earthly Branch
Chia	Yin
Yi	Mao
Ping	Ch'en
Ting	Szu
Wu	Wu
Chi	Wei
Keng	Shen
Hsin	Yu
Jen	Hsu
Kuei	Hai

Heavenly Stem	Earthly Branch
Chia	Hsu
Yi	Hai
Ping	Tzu
Ting	Ch'ou
Wu	Yin
Chi	Mao
Keng	Ch'en
Hsin	Szu
Jen	Wu
Kuei	Wei

Heavenly Stem	Earthly Branch
Chia	Ch'en
Yi	Szu
Ping	Wu
Ting	Wei
Wu	Shen
Chi	Yu
Keng	Hsu
Hsin	Hai
Jen	Tzu
Kuei	Ch'ou

Heavenly Stem	Earthly Branch
Chia	Wu
Yi	Wei
Ping	Shen
Ting	Yu
Wu	Hsu
Chi	Hai
Keng	Tzu
Hsin	Ch'ou
Jen	Yin
Kuei	Mao

Heavenly Stem	Earthly Branch
Chia	Shen
Yi	Yu
Ping	Hsu
Ting	Hai
Wu	Tzu
Chi	Ch'ou
Keng	Yin
Hsin	Mao
Jen	Ch'en
Kuei	Szu

The Sixty Year Cycle

The Jade Emperor and the Twelve Animals
One day the Jade Emperor was bored of life in Heaven, and as he idly gazed towards the earth he wondered what the creatures of that land looked like. Now that his curiosity was aroused, he summoned one of his assistants:

'Go down to the earth and order the creatures to visit me in the palace'.

'But there are so many, your majesty, do you want me to bring them all?', replied the assistant.

'No, I only want to see the most interesting. Select twelve and bring them to me as soon as you can.'

The assistant travelled to earth and gave his first invitation to a rat. 'When you see your friend, the cat, ask him to come to the palace. I know that emperor will be fascinated by his coat.'

The assistant then continued on his journey and along the way he sent invitations to the ox, the tiger, the rabbit, the dragon, the snake, the horse, the ram, the monkey, the cock and the dog, telling them to be at the palace at six o'clock the next morning.

The animals preened themselves in preparation and the rat dutifully went in search of the cat. The cat was delighted to hear the news but since he was a deep sleeper, he made the rat promise to wake him up early the next morning. The rat gave his promise and then returned to his nest to sleep. But the rat couldn't sleep and the more he thought about the cat, the more jealous he became.

'That cat is far too beautiful, he will outshine me', he thought to himself. And as the night wore on the rat decided not to wake the cat.

The next morning eleven animals were lined up for inspection in the palace courtyard. The Jade Emperor walked slowly past each one and when he came to the end of the line he turned to his assistant. 'They are fine creatures, but where is the twelfth one? I want the last animal here immediately', demanded the king.

Afraid that he may lose his position in the palace the assistant returned to earth at full speed to find a substitute for the cat. The first thing that caught his eye was a servant carrying a pig through a farmyard and so the assistant took the pig to the parade.

Meanwhile the rat was still anxious to be noticed and so he sat on the ox's back and played a flute. The king was fascinated by this unusual creature and gave him first place. The ox was placed second since he had been generous enough to allow the rat to sit on his back. The courageous-looking tiger was placed third and the rabbit with his fine white hair was placed fourth. The king thought the dragon resembled a strong snake on legs and so he was given fifth place. The snake was given sixth, the horse seventh, the ram eighth, the monkey ninth, the cock tenth and the dog eleventh. The king considered the pig the ugliest of all the assembled animals, but he had no choice but to give him twelfth place. No sooner had the king made these awards than the cat ran into the palace.

'I'm sorry, your majesty, I overslept but I beg you now to give me a chance.'

But it was too late, the king had already made his decision on the twelve animals of the horoscope and their corresponding twelve earthly branches. The cat accepted his fate but he could never quite forgive the rat, and to this day the cat still bears that grudge.

The Chinese day is traditionally broken into twelve hours, each hour corresponds to two ordinary hours. The chart opposite shows how each animal was attributed a year, a time of day, a period within the year and a direction.

When the Heavenly Stems, Earthly Branches and four trigrams appear on the compass to mark the twenty-four directional points (see pages 42 and 43), they are not only used for marking the positions of the dragon ch'i and of watercourses, but they are used also for marking lucky and unlucky points. The stems can be used as numerals 1 to 10. Stems 1, 2, 9, and 10 are unlucky; stems 3, 4, 7, and 8 are lucky. Stems 5 and 6 are at the centre of the compass and not on this directional ring. They are said to be unlucky

Earthly branch	Animal	Period of the Year	Hour	Direction
T-zu	rat	mid-winter	11pm–1am	N
Ch'ou	ox	end of winter	1am–3am	NNE
Yin	tiger	early spring	3am–5am	ENE
Mao	rabbit	mid-spring	5am–7am	E
Ch'en	dragon	end of spring	7am–9am	ESE
Szu	snake	early summer	9am–11am	SSE
Wu	horse	mid-summer	11am–1pm	S
Wei	ram	end of summer	1pm–3pm	SSW
Shen	monkey	early autumn	3pm–5pm	WSW
Yu	cock	mid-autumn	5pm–7pm	W
Hsu	dog	end of autumn	7pm–9pm	WNW
Hai	pig	early winter	9pm–11pm	NNW

Heavenly stems	Number	Direction in the 24 points	Luck
Chia	1	ENE by E	bad
Yi	2	ESE by E	bad
Ping	3	SSE by S	good
Ting	4	SSW by S	good
Wu	5		
		Centre	bad
Chi	6		
Keng	7	WSW by W	good
Hsin	8	WNW by W	good
Jen	9	NNW by N	bad
Kuei	10	NNE by N	bad

but they are capable of dispersing the positive energy of ch'i over areas where malign forces have accumulated.

The elements are placed at interim stages to indicate their interaction between the various aspects of the stems.

THE EIGHT CHARACTER HOROSCOPE

Before giving a reading of a site the geomancer must, at the very least, know the birth date of the person concerned. Using the Pa Che method (see chapter 4), their corresponding element, hexagram and auspicious directions can be calculated. For greater accuracy, he may produce an eight character horoscope using the stems and branches that correspond to the hour, date, month and year of birth. The days and months, like the years, follow a cycle of sixty, and the stems and branches rotate accordingly. The stems and branches allocated to the hours follow a fixed pattern.

CH'I

Ch'i is commonly referred to as the life breath. The geomancer's skill lies in his ability to allow for the unhindered circulation of this energy in relation to dwellings of the living and of the dead.

The main purpose of ch'i is to function as the principle shaping all forms. This function is described by the philosopher Chu Hsi:

> Throughout heaven and earth there is Li and there is Ch'i. Li is the Tao (organising) all forms from above, and the root from which all things are produced. Ch'i is the instrument (composing) all forms from below, and the tools and raw materials with which all things are made. Thus men and all other things must receive this Li at the moment of their

coming into being, and thus get their specific nature; so also must they receive this Ch'i and thus get their form.[4]

While li determines order, ch'i animates it so that it is capable of physical being – they are interdependent, one cannot exist without the other. A feng shui expert is concerned with the place where ch'i accumulates, because this will confer fortune on those who live and those who are buried there. When referred to in its plural form, ch'i is identified with yin and yang as they operate in the changing of the seasons, in the climate and in the landscape. Ch'i comes and goes in a continuous flow, prospering and dispersing, growing and decaying. The continual and often irregular accumulation and dispersal of ch'i at certain points on the ground is known as 'earth ch'i'. The stages of ch'i at any time or place on the ground can be identified by the geomancer using the information on the compass dial.

The ch'i that govern the regular cosmic cycle of seasons are known as 'heaven ch'i'. Besides the division of the year into four seasons, the annual cycle is broken into six phases, known as 'heaven ch'i'. The six phases do not fall at regular intervals, according to the year some are more pronounced than others. The phases are further divided into twenty-four terms which mark solar, climatic and agricultural patterns. These phases occur every 15–16 days, and are described in detail on page 46.

There is yet another aspect of ch'i that is related to the earth, but is not part of it as earth ch'i is. This is ch'i in the literal sense of the life breath or energy that courses through the earth – the arteries and veins of the dragon – and through its rivers and streams. By observing the lie of the land, the geomancer can observe where ch'i are accumulating. Shallow, fast-flowing rivers or streams disperse ch'i, as do hills exposed to strong winds. These are the places where yang accumulates. Low-lying valleys and pools of water encourage ch'i, they are sources of peace and quiet and a reflection of yin. The ch'i identified here in the broad sweep of the landscape is different to readings taken on the compass to identify ch'i at specific points on the ground.

Ch'i produce life but they are also subject to decay and their absence or weakness in an area or spot will allow sha, the life-taking breaths, to enter. Sha can appear as the result of one element overpowering or destroying another causing sickness, business failure, family arguments, marital disputes, or impotence.

Sha in its physical sense is manifest in the cold wind that blows from the earth through hollows in the land and in wind that pierces gaps in ridges or outcrops that protect a site. Sha that takes life and distributes malign influences can be found anywhere. This type of sha travels along straight lines, natural or man-made. A corner of a building facing onto a railway line, telephone line or straight watercourse is considered bad feng shui. The ideal site is protected and peaceful but open to gentle winds that allow ch'i to circulate. This site should be southfacing. A southfacing site is particularly important in China since it will benefit from warm, wet winds and will be protected from bitter northern winds. A building or a grave should be built in a hollow on a gentle slope so that air can circulate freely. The soil should be well-drained but not hard or rocky, and a pool of water lower down the slope will not only improve drainage but will also encourage the accumulation of ch'i. Well-drained soil is also required for the preservation of the coffin, and, more importantly, for the preservation of the bones. Finding a site that affords good bone and coffin preservation is seen by the Chinese as a filial duty. This is how an ideal grave site is described:

> Near the surface, one half should be sand and one half clay, with but few large stones. After digging four or five feet you may come upon a rock that cannot be moved, or upon water, and the place has to be abandoned. At a depth of three or four feet a layer of clay may be reached, and at six or seven feet a layer of sand, then a layer of loose stones, and then a layer of hard clay, yellow, red or variegated. Beyond this, water will be

reached. Those buried above the hard clay find the air warm and comfortable, and have no trouble from water or white ants. Good clay is a sure indication that it is a safe place to bury, and the quantity of the clay may be tested by taking bits from the side and straining it through water. If no sand appears and the clay feels greasy to the touch, it is good.[5]

Besides the practical benefits, a well-placed site will bring good health, family harmony and successful trading. A site that is pleasing to the eye and peaceful to live in, which receives the sun and has an unrestricted view of natural features, will no doubt encourage emotional well-being. Details outlining the advantages and hazards of choosing building sites, domestic or commercial premises are outlined in chapters 5–8.

3 · THE LANDSCAPE AND THE COMPASS

The symbols inscribed on the compass ring are rarely static since the forces in the landscape are in a continual state of flux. The symbols reflect the carefully balanced relationship between heaven and earth, the tension and opposition between yin and yang, elements, hexagrams, stars, and the hundreds of other symbols of the compass. Even within a single series of symbols, one symbol refers to another and interacts with it.

In practical terms this constant interaction is applied to five basic landscape categories:

Shan

This is the dragon, the most important feature of the land since it can create or destroy human fortune. The dragon is linear in that it links every shape in the landscape to a line of other shapes. The twists, turns and curves of its body can be seen in all topographical formations. Hills, mountain ridges and formations are the dragon's veins and arteries through which ch'i, the dragon's blood, can circulate. Water courses are the dragon's ducts though which the water ch'i can flow.

As with a human body, the dragon's body also has capillaries and ducts which carry ch'i but if there are too many small channels around a site the ch'i is easily dispersed. The higher the concentration of ch'i through the veins or arteries, the greater the fortune bestowed on the site. The geomancer can identify where the dragon influence enters or leaves, disperses or leaks, condenses or collects. He is also able to determine the type of dragon – whether it is straight, lying across a site, or riding a site. The point at which the forces in the landscape have a powerful and positive effect is called the dragon point.

Shui

Shui refers to watercourses or pools flowing through or situated close to the site. Sluggish or stagnant water can affect the fortune of the site since it is a place where sha will accumulate. The quality and the movement of the water is also an indication of the soil type in the area.

Sha

Sha is the term for formations of earth, mud or sand and is a term applied to unusual land or riverbank formations.

Chai

Chai is the site itself or the dwelling, whether it is a house, tomb or office.

Hsueh

Hsueh is the 'lair' of the dragon and also refers to the site, particularly if it is in a well-protected place such as a hollow or a site shielded on three sides.

LO' PAN – THE COMPASS

This introduction to the compass is based on a simple nine ringed compass which contains the basic information a geomancer may need. To give an accurate reading, the geomancer correlates the symbols and information given in each ring with the horoscope details of the individual.

In order to take the bearings of a site or a feature of the landscape the geomancer holds the compass or places it against the straight side of an object aligned with the direction

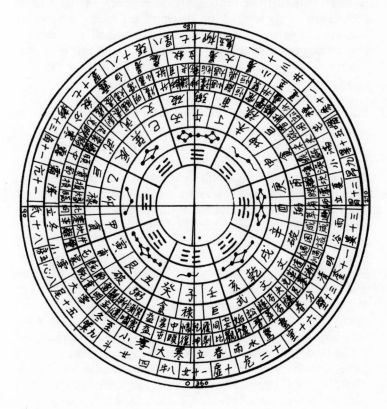

Lo Pan – The Compass

from which he wishes to take a reading. The compass is set on a square base to make this possible. There are two threads held taut which cross at the centre of the compass and the geomancer positions the compass so that one of these threads is directly in line with the direction he is facing. The dial listing the concentric circles is moved around until it is aligned with the needle. A reading can then be taken along the line of symbols that appear under the line of the thread.

The centre of the compass is known as Heaven's Pool or Tai Chi. The area is divided in half by a magnetic needle. It is believed that the compass provides order for life and in the middle is the well of the Heaven Pool where action and rest work together. The Heaven Pool symbolically represents the starting point of ch'i, the life breath. It is in this Pool that the forces of yin and yang can divide and interact with each other, when one ascends, the other declines, and so they work and rest in harmony. Their action in turn gives rise to the elements and other forms and forces. The Heaven pool is regarded as the centre of the universe.

The first ring contains the original trigrams devised by Fu Hsi (see p.23). The Former Heaven trigrams are laid out among the eight points of the compass. Within this sequence, the forces of yin and yang wax and wane. Yang is at its greatest in ch'ien, the southern and most male trigram, and yin is at its strongest in K'un, the northern and most female trigram. This movement from strength to weakness through the trigrams of the Former Heaven sequence represents the cycle of the seasons from winter, when yin is at its peak, through spring and onto summer, when yang is at its peak and then the yin forces build up again through autumn to culminate in winter.

The second ring contains the symbols of the nine stars which move through the cosmos affecting the fate of humans. When the stars are moving they are invisible, when they can be seen they are believed to be the seven stars of the Dipper plus two nearby stars. These nine stars also correspond to the nine different compass readings given in the Pa Che system described in chapter 4.

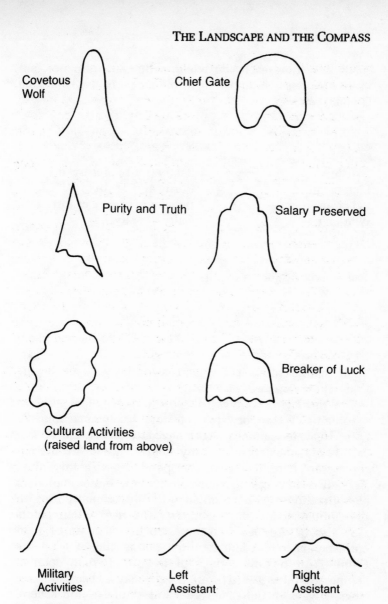

The Nine Stars reflected in the formations of mountains and hills

Not only does each star wield a different influence, but its presence is also apparent in the shape of the land. The Dipper stars are:

T'an lung	Covetous wolf
Chu-men	Chief gate
Lu-ts'un	Salary (rank) preserved
Lien-chen	Purity and Truth
P'o-chun	Breaker of armies or fortune
Wen-ch'u	Cultural activities
Wu-ch'u	Military activities

The remaining stars are:

Tso-fu	Left assistant
Yu-pi	Right assistant

Their manifestation in the land is loosely covered by the forms shown on page 41.

The third ring follows the position of the twenty-four mountains. These correspond to four hexagrams from the Later Heaven sequence, eight heavenly stems and twelve earthly branches. The heavenly stems Wu and Chi are not represented here since they correspond to earth at the centre. As well as having a symbolic meaning, the mountains are also directional points similar to the directional points on the sundial or mariner's compass. The twenty-four points may also be grouped into threes so that a group of eight corresponds to the four cardinal points and to what the Chinese call the four 'corners' of the earth. In more detailed compasses these twenty-four points may appear in three rings, always in the same order but shifted round several degrees. The three rings correlate to Heaven, Earth, and Man, all are equally effective and must act in harmony with one another to maintain the balance of the universe.

Branches	Trigrams	Stems	Direction
		jen	NNW by N
tzu			N
		kuei	NNE by N
ch'ou			NNE by E
	ken		NE
yin			ENE by N
		chia	ENE by E
mao			E
		yi	ESE by E
ch'en			ESE by S
	sun		SE
szu			SSE by E
		ping	SSE by S
wu			S
		ting	SSW by S
wei			SSW by W
	k'un		SW
shen			WSW by S
		keng	WSW by W
yu			W
		hsin	WNW by W
hsu			WNW by N
	ch'ien		NW
hai			NNW by W

When readings are taken from the three rings each symbol's influence is slightly blurred and it allows for a greater interaction with neighbouring symbols. Although this indicates a continual state of flux within the symbols, the cardinal points are considered to be unchanging and the 'corner' points changing. The symbols are arranged as shown in the table above.

The fourth ring lists the eight major Tzu Wei stars from the Tzu Wei astrology system. Tzu Wei is the name of the god in charge of what is variously called the Purple Planet, the Purple Star or the Pole Star. The Pole Star is the centre of the astronomical system and the astrological calendar. Ursa Major and Ursa Minor, the two closest constellations are seen as the North and South Measures which represent a human lifespan. The god of birth dwells in the Southern Measure and the god of death in the Northern Measure. The Pole Star is the centre of life and the stars that surround it are measured in relation to this central star. Each of the eight stars in this ring appears four times which gives the geomancer the opportunity to choose alternative positions if one aspect gives an inauspicious reading.

The fifth and sixth rings each contain the sixty-four hexagrams (the sixty-four possible combinations that arise from combining the eight trigrams). Since all things are subject to change, except the Tao, the hexagrams listed in the fifth ring provide a reading for the present, the sixth ring provides a reading for what may happen in the future.

The Sixty-four hexagrams

Ch'ien	The origin	Tun	To hide
K'un	Success	Ta Chuang	Great strength
Chun	Birth pangs	Chin	To advance
Meng	Rebellious youth	Ming I	Brightness dimmed
Hsu	Patience	Chia Jen	The family
Sung	Contention	K'uei	Opposition
Shih	The army	Chien	Obstruction
Pi	Unity	Hsieh	Let loose
Hsiao Ch'u	Holding back the less able	Sun	Injured
Li	Walking carefully	I	Increase
		Kuai	New outcome
		Kou	To meet
T'ai	Benevolence	Ts'ui	To collect
P'i	Obstruction	Sheng	Rising up
T'ung Jen	Companions	K'un	To surround

44

Ta Yu	Many possessions		and wear out
		Ching	The well
Ch'ien	Modesty	Ko	Change
Yu	Enthusiasm	Ting	The cooking
Sui	According or agreeing with		pot
		Chen	Shock
Ku	Decay	Ken	Resting
Lin	To draw near	Chien	Gradual
Kuan	Examine		development
Shih Ho	Biting through	Kuei Mei	Marrying the
Pi	To adorn		younger sister
Po	Peeling or splitting	Feng	Prosperity
		Lu	The traveller
Fu	Return	Sun	Gentle and
Wu Wang	Not false		yielding
Ta Ch'u	Great domesticating powers	Tui	Happiness
		Huan	Scattered
		Chieh	Limitations
I	Taking nourishment	Chung Fu	Inner confidence
Ta Kuo	Great experience	Hsaio Kou	Minor problems
K'an	Watery depths	Chi Chi	Already done
Li	To shine brightly, to part	Wei Chi	Not yet done
Hsien	All embracing		
Heng	Constant		

The seventh ring contains the twenty-four terms of the solar calendar. These twenty-four phases were and still are used by farmers to guide them through the agricultural year. Each of the twenty-four terms corresponds to 15° of the sun's motion in longitude on the ecliptic and in the calendar they occur every fifteen or sixteen days. Although this solar calendar is correlated with the other rings on the compass, it does not have the symbolic value of the other rings and is used purely for practical reasons. This cycle indicates to the geomancer the periods of growth and decay and it is divided into

8 chieh and 16 chi. Chi indicates the periods of growth and decay, which in a greater sense is part of what yin and yang represent. Chieh mark the end of certain periods and herald the beginning of new phases in the annual cycle.

The twenty-four terms of the solar calendar

Chieh	Li Ch'un	Beginning of spring
Ch'i	Yu Shui	Rain water
Ch'i	Ching Chi	Excited insects
Chieh	Ch'un Fen	Spring equinox
Ch'i	Ch'ing Ming	Clear and bright
Ch'i	Ku Yu	Grain rains
Chieh	Li Hsia	Summer begins
Ch'i	Hsaio Man	Grain filling
Ch'i	Mang Chung	Grain in ear
Chieh	Hsai Chi	Summer solstice
Ch'i	Hsiao Shu	Slight heat
Ch'i	Ta Shu	Great heat
Chieh	Li Ch'iu	Autumn begins
Ch'i	Ch'u Shu	Limit of heat
Ch'i	Pai Lu	White dew
Chieh	Ch'iu Fen	Autumn equinox
Ch'i	Han Lu	Cold dew
Ch'i	Shuang Chiang	Hoar frost descends
Chieh	Li Tung	Winter begins
Ch'i	Hsaio Hsueh	Slight snow
Ch'i	Ta Hsueh	Great snow
Chieh	Tung Chih	Winter solstice
Ch'i	Hsiao Han	Slight cold
Ch'i	Ta Han	Great cold

The eighth ring contains the twenty-eight constellations which are used for determining the position and time of the burial. The constellations are usually gathered into groups of seven to represent the four quarters of the compass. The constellations or hsui were asterims distributed around the celestial equator in 2400 BCE although their positions have changed so that they can no longer be regarded, if they originally were, as points marking the equator. The constellations are all visible throughout the year so each is considered to govern twenty-eight differently sized portions of a circle with Heaven at the centre. Constellations can bestow good luck or misfortune on a certain day, so if the first reading is unsuitable the geomancer can refer to the yearly almanac to check the annual movement of the constellation in question and determine an alternative date that offers a positive reading.

The ninth ring divides up the 360° of the circle. Prior to the arrival of the Jesuits in China during the sixteenth and seventeenth centuries bringing with them advanced astrological techniques, the Chinese circle was divided into 365 ¼°.

A THIRTY-SIX-RINGED COMPASS

There are no set rules for the number of rings on a compass or their content, although it is unusual to find a compass with more than thirty-eight rings. The compass illustrated on page 49 has thirty-six rings and their names and purposes are described in the list that follows:

1. Fu Hsi hexagrams – (former hexagrams)
2. Wen Wang hexagrams – (later hexagrams)
3. The eight positions of the Baleful Spirits – help identify unlucky positions on the ground.
4. The four and eight ways of Wang Ch'uen – these are used to help find the deceased an auspicious position in the land of the dead so as to ensure a good rebirth.
5. The Nine Star and Separating the Dragon Ring – these are used to identify whether the dragon is lucky or malign on the land or rivers surrounding the grave.

6. The Earth Valley Needle – this is the opposite of the Heaven Pool. It is used in the cemetery to find the most suitable position for the tombstone.

7. Yin and Yang Dragon Ring – this contains the heavenly stems and earthly branches.

8. The twenty-four Mountains and the five Dragons (elements) – the geomancer uses this ring to identify the elements which attack or help the deceased.

9. The Baleful and Evil Ring – this identifies the spirits in the land that may cause misfortune or accidents within the family of the deceased.

10. The seventy-two points of the Dragon through the Mountain – the geomancer takes a reading from a hill to check the dragon ch'i coming from the hill in relation to the site.

11. Through the Mountain Later hexagrams – this is used to develop the reading taken from ring 10. This reading is also taken from a hill to determine auspicious points on the site within the range of the hexagram.

12. The Human Pool – this is used at the site to assess the horoscope of the living and occasionally the dead to determine if it is compatible with the eight character horoscope of the person concerned. Readings are taken of the hexagrams, stems and branches. If a feng shui diagnosis is taken at the grave the geomancer is able to comment on how the position of the deceased can affect the fortune of the family.

13. The Earth Spirit of the sixty Dragons – this is used to discover the points where the earth spirits help or attack so that the coffin can be placed in a good position.

14. Through the Earth Door – this ring finds the right path for the dead to travel through the earth to the land of the spirits, Wang Ch'uen.

15. Through the Earth and Mountain hexagrams – these are used to assess which hexagrams are compatible with the Dragon points in the earth and in the mountain.

16. Through the Earth Dragon – is combined with the twenty-eight constellations. Using the position of the dragon and the

羅經透解全圖

羅經

A 36 ringed Compass

第一層　先天八卦
第二層　洛書即後天卦
第三層　八煞黃泉、
第四層　四路八路黃泉
第五層　九星分龍貴賤
第六層　地盤正針
第七層　地盤正針
第八層　陰陽龍
第九層　二十四山正五龍
第十層　刻煞盤
第十一層　穿山七十二龍
第十二層　穿山周易卦
第十三層　中針人盤
第十四層　透地六十龍連偏正盤
第十五層　透地奇門
第十六層　透地連山卦
第十七層　透地龍配二十八宿

貴人祿馬子父財官此盤字
終羅經六更刻象青見畫言

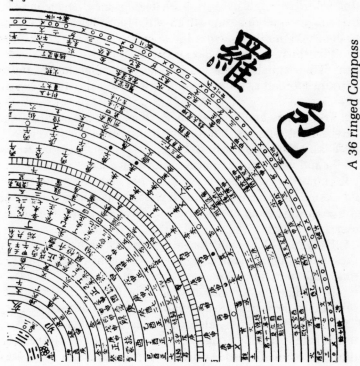

49

twenty-eight constellations the geomancer can identify good or bad positions for the burial.

17. The Astrology Ring – is used to check the balance of the elements, yin and yang, stems, branches and hexagrams so that a full horoscope reading can be taken at the site and in relation to the person concerned.

18. The Heaven Pool Adjusting Needle – this ring takes into account all the readings taken so far. This ring is usually marked with different coloured sections to denote yin and yang divisions on the compass.

19. The 246° of the compass ring – is used to take a reading at 246° to the headstone so that the lay of the land and the courses of rivers can be read at that point.

20. The 28° of the deceased – if the geomancer is unable to find a positive angle using ring 19, he then uses the degrees of this ring to find the best position of the tombstone in relation to the rivers and land forms.

21. The thirty-seven Angles of the Deceased – are used to calculate a suitable position for the tombstone taking into account footpaths, rivers, roads, spirits and the circulation of ch'i.

22. The Lonely and Prosperous Positions for the Dead – the fifty-nine hexagrams that appear in this ring are correlated with the position of the burial site, the elements, the balance of yin and yang and the horoscope of the deceased.

23. The hexagrams appear again so that once the geomancer has found a suitable angle for the site he can check against the relevant hexagram to ensure it is in harmony with the deceased.

24. Heavenly Stems and Earthly Branches combine to find the five elements – since the elements change according to the combinations of stems and branches, this ring is used to check that the element associated with stem and branch relevant to the burial are compatible with the deceased.

25. The twelve Islands, also known as the twelve Palaces – used to identify which palace is associated with the deceased. (Each palace deals with a different aspect of person. They are

the Ming palace, Brothers and Sisters palace, Marital palace, Man and Woman palace, Wealth palace, Sickness palace, Moving palace, Servants palace, Officials palace, Property palace, Fortune and Virtue palace, Parents palace.)

26. The Life Star Ring – used to discover the life star or constellation of the deceased. The constellations in this ring do not direct or control the fate of the deceased.

27. The twenty-four Mountains – used to identify the angle at which the sun rises in relation to the grave.

28. The three Generals on Duty – the names of these three powerful spirits and guardians are repeated around the ring and one will be in charge of the deceased.

29. The twelve Gods in Command – these correlate with the twelve palaces of ring 25.

30. The Horse Palace Ring – the Horse is the travelling star which appears in thirty-one positions. The position of the star in relation to the grave will indicate whether the soul of the deceased will wander or be content and comfortable. This is important since the condition of the deceased will affect the fortunes of the family.

32. The Heaven Degree Ring – this is used to discover the element that corresponds to the Heavenly Spirit that enters the point at which the reading is taken.

33. The 10° of the sixty Dragon Points – once the geomancer has identified a suitable angle, he will automatically read the 10° that span that position. The 10° then correlate with one of the sixty dragon points.

34. This ring indicates the latitude and longitude of the site.

35. When the ten Heavenly Stems and the twelve Earthly Branches are combined there are always two branches left over, and this ring lists the dead branches at various positions. The geomancer is able to check that the dead branches associated with the direction of the site do not appear in the eight character horoscope of the person concerned.

36. The twenty-eight constellations that appear in this ring do not direct or control the deceased. They are used by the geomancer to correlate a constellation with the burial site of the deceased.

THE GEOMANCER'S RULER

The exact proportions of a building, room or the height of furniture should be checked by the geomancer to ensure fortune and prosperity. To do this he uses a geomancer's ruler that not only marks distances but also implies lucky or unlucky measurements.

The Chinese characters above the centimetres are for internal use, those marked under the inches are for external use. The characters that are written in the boxes indicate whether this is a lucky or unlucky measurement. At the end of the fourth box of characters on the internal and external markings the category of fortune changes, for example the first four boxes marked on the external line in the diagram opposite represent different aspects of wealth and the four boxes that follow it represent different aspects of loss and disease. There is a character written in the middle of each group of four which denotes the overall fortune for that group. At the end of thirty-two boxes of characters on the external line and forty boxes of characters on the internal line the characters are repeated once again.

1. *Readings from the lower line used for the internal measurements:*

1–4	Harm
5–8	Prosperity
9–12	Distress
13–16	Reason
17–20	Official title
21–24	Death
25–28	Expansion
29–32	Loss
33–36	Wealth
37–40	Children

The Geomancers Ruler

2. *Readings from the upper line used for external measurements:*

1–4	Wealth
5–8	Disease
9–12	Leaving
13–16	Reason
17–20	Title
21–24	Robbery
25–28	Harm
29–32	Capital

THE LO SHU MAGIC SQUARE AND NUMBERS

Other numerical calculations used by the geomancer in his assessment are based on the Lo Shu magical square. Traditionally, Chinese cities and temples were laid out in a square broken into nine sections, a layout based on the concept of the Lo Shu magical square. This square was believed to have been revealed to the legendary emperor Yu by a turtle who emerged from the river Lo. Yu was the first man to control the flow of the mighty river Lo and was rewarded with knowledge of the magic square for his engineering skill.

Ta Yu had worked for the government for thirteen years as an inspector of ditches, dykes, and water courses. He was respected for his knowledge and patience and many believed Heaven had blessed him with a great wisdom. Whenever a river broke its banks or new ditches had to be built in complicated terrain Ta Yu was summoned for his judgement.

Along its course the river Lo flowed through Shansi province and as it approached the north side of Dragon Gate mountain, its waters became turbulent, and deep, dangerous, whirlpools formed in its course so the fields were flooded. Many had been unexpectedly caught in its torrents and as soon as Dragon Gate mountain appeared in view the boats were hauled out of the water, but for some it was too late. When the river Lo reached the mountainside, huge waves lashed its sides, and long ago the trees had been uprooted by the force of the river and boulders tossed across the land. Once the river Lo had reached the mountain it followed a dangerous course around its base and continued on its south side.

The governor of Shansi province decided that the only man who might be able to tame the powerful river was Ta Yu and he was ordered to build a tunnel through Dragon Gate Mountain linking the north and south sides. Ta Yu spent many days surveying the site and once he had decided where to begin hollowing out the tunnel he asked for three hundred men and twenty cartloads of tools and equipment. During the ensuing weeks the men laboured on attempting to build the hollow for the tunnel, and many were thrown to their deaths in the water or killed by falling rocks. As each man died another was sent on to take his place. Ta Yu worked alongside the men each day, willing to put his own life at risk too, and in the evening, when the day's work had finished, he remained at the site assessing the work and making new plans.

After six months and the loss of more than a hundred lives a tunnel had finally been dug from the north to the south side of the mountain and the flow of the mighty river had been controlled. One evening, after he had examined the structure of the tunnel, Ta Yu followed a path up the mountain that he had never seen before. Suddenly the evening sun warmed his limbs but then, in the next moment, a cold wind passed over him. As he looked up, he saw an entrance to a cave that wasn't marked on the plans he had made. He entered a huge cavern, and guided by shafts of light that fell through narrow slits in the stone he came to a narrow path at the back of the cavern. The light had begun to fade, and it was too dark to see the way ahead, so Ta Yu unwillingly turned back and left the cave.

The next morning, armed with an oil lamp, Ta Yu retraced his steps and once more entered the path that led from the cavern, deep into the mountain. He noticed strange lines and diagrams carved in the damp walls of the passage and unexpectedly his light fell across the sleeping form of an animal. At first he thought it was a pig, but its skin had a faint yellow tinge and it held a bright, perfectly rounded pearl in its mouth.

Ta Yu stepped across the animal's body and continued until he caught sight of a fierce dog, crouching low as though ready to pounce. He stood perfectly still but the dog only barked as though trying to speak to him. The dog rose to its feet, span on its heels and loped on deeper into the mountain. Ta Yu then heard a movement from behind and turned to see the yellow pig standing close behind him. He had no choice but to follow the dog.

He walked along with them for countless miles and although he had had nothing to eat or drink for a long time he felt exhilarated. It was only when he caught sight of a bright white light ahead of him that his limbs suddenly felt heavy and his body exhausted.

Without warning, the dog stopped, turned to face Ta Yu and fixed him with piercing, green eyes. Ta Yu was transfixed and unable to see the pig who had slowly begun to take the shape of a man in flowing, black robes. Then as he watched, the dog's fore and hind legs began to assume the shape of human limbs and gradually he, too, became a man in black robes. It was then that Ta Yu knew that his guards were the Jade Emperor's servants. A figure appeared ahead in a bright circle of light and Ta Yu was drawn to him. The creature had the face of a snake but the body of a man and Ta Yu knew he was in the presence of a deity. He lifted a parchment scroll from the floor beside him and beckoned Ta Yu to come closer. Eight groups of lines had been drawn in black ink on the scroll, some were straight and others broken. The creature had revealed the eight trigrams to Ta Yu.

'Are you the sage, the son of Wah Su?' asked Ta Yu.

'I am,' he replied, 'my mother was born and lived in a perfect land. One day a rainbow appeared and she stood in its light for two hours. The Jade Emperor sent a baby down the rainbow and after twelve years she gave birth to me.'

Ta Yu thought back to the legends he had learnt as a child and realised he was in the presence of a great Emperor famed for his wise rule throughout China. The Emperor then offered Ta Yu a jade tablet twelve units in length. Each unit represented the twelve divisions of the day and of the year. He then handed him a turtle shell inscribed with the Lo Shu magic square. Ta Yu bowed low and accepted his gifts. Finally the emperor spoke,

'You have shown great wisdom and skill in taming the river Lo. The tunnel through the Dragon Gate mountain was your final test; you have proved yourself worthy of ruling China. The hexagrams on the scroll will help you to predict the auspicious years for your people, the jade tablet gives you the authority to govern wisely, the inscriptions on the turtle shell give you the ability to plan well.

Cradling the precious gifts in his arms, Ta Yu left the emperor and returned to the outside world. As the emperor had predicted, Ta Yu was praised throughout China for his engineering feats and was soon declared Emperor. According to legend, the Emperor Yu reigned for forty years and during his wise rule the land was never plagued by drought, flood or famine.

The even, female or yin numbers are placed at the corner of the square and the odd, male or yang numbers are at the four cardinal points and the centre. Nine and one are considered the most auspicious numbers since nine represents wholeness, something that is complete, and one is the beginning of all things. If the numbers are added up in any line they come to fifteen. The square is based on an earlier design that incorporated a central fifth square. Many cities not only in China but also in Egypt, India and in Ireland were based on this principle. The four quarters represented the four seasons and the four quarters of the city and the central square the seat of government and guidance.

The simple square with a central fifth square probably developed into the square with nine divisions on the basis of a hand count. The little finger down to the thumb are the odd numbers 1, 3, 5, 7 and 9 and the hollows between the fingers and the thumb are the even numbers 2, 4, 6 and 8. The number 5 at the centre is the most powerful, it is translated as 'wu' in Chinese and the Chinese characters for 'midday' and for 'myself' are also read as 'wu'.

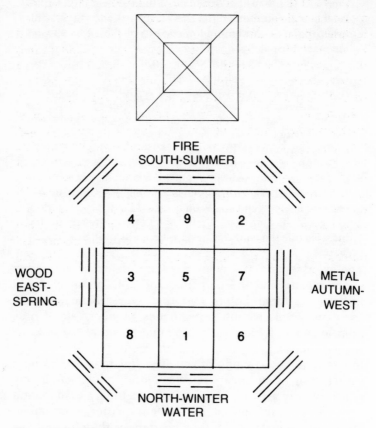

The Lo Shu Magic Square

The Lo Shu magical square is also a diagramatic representation of the seasons. The numbers, followed in a clockwise direction, show the ratio of yang to yin in the annual cycle. In winter yang is at its lowest (1) and yin at its highest (8) and in the summer yang is at its highest (9) and yin its lowest (2). The square also orders the trigrams of the Later Heaven sequence and the elements according to the compass directions.

58

Aware of the power inherent in the Lo Shu magic square, architects and geomancers advised their rulers to build cities, temples, palaces and mansions to this plan. The Imperial Palace in Peking is based on this square, and in feudal times the landowner who could afford nine rooms followed this layout, moving from room to room according to the seasons so that his rule over his subjects was wisely regulated.

Even though planning according to the Lo Shu square does not exert such a powerful influence in modern day planning the association with lucky and unlucky numbers is still effective in Chinese life. Numbers themselves or hononyms – words which have similar pronunciation – have an important bearing on personal or business decisions. If the numbers in the time or date of a wedding or signing a contract added up to nine this would be considered lucky but numbers adding up to four or ending in four are considered unlucky since the Cantonese word for four sounds like the word 'die'.

4 · THE PA CHE SYSTEM

A PERSONAL COMPASS

The Pa Che system uses the later trigrams to determine the nine directions and each individual's life will match one of these directions. The charts in this chapter enable the reader to determine his or her own favourable directions from the nine variations of the Pa Che compass and to identify the directions where good or malign spirits have influence. Once you have calculated the number of your compass there are tables which list the colours most appropriate to your nature and the elements which can cause harmony or chaos in your life.

Pa Che feng shui is divided into two groups known as the eastern life and the western life. In an eastern life southern, southeastern, east and northern directions bring good fortune. In a western life western, north-west, south-west and north-east bring good fortune. If, after making the calculations below, you discover that you have an eastern life, live in an eastern house. If your main door faces to the east you will have the most auspicious forecast, however, if these directions clash the harmony of your life is disrupted.

DETERMINING YOUR OWN PA CHE COMPASS

In the following system, each one of the nine directions which corresponds to a trigram and to an element is given a number. These numbers, which are said to have been revealed through the mysterious forces of Heaven are contained in the *Book of River-Lo* and the *Plan of the Yellow River*. Although there are only eight trigrams, there are nine directions, since the centre is considered one of the directions. In this system K'un and K'en are repeated so that they align with the centre which corresponds to number 5. If after making your calculations you end up with the number 5, you will discover from the illustrated compass below that the centre does not have its own particular forecast although it is an essential direction. A man who calculates the number 5 should follow the reading that corresponds to K'un, number 2, and a woman should follow the reading which corresponds to Ken, number 8.

HOW TO FIND YOUR DIRECTIONAL NUMBER

CALCULATIONS FOR MEN

Subtract your year of birth from 100 and divide by nine. The remainder is your number. If there is no remainder you must take the number 9.

Example: For a man born in 1960

$100 - 60 = 40$ divided by 9 = 4 with a remainder of 4.

The reading is contained in the compass surrounding number 4.

Example: For a man born in 1955

$100 - 55 = 45$ divided by 9 = 5.

Since there is no remainder the correct reading is found in the compass surrounding number 9.

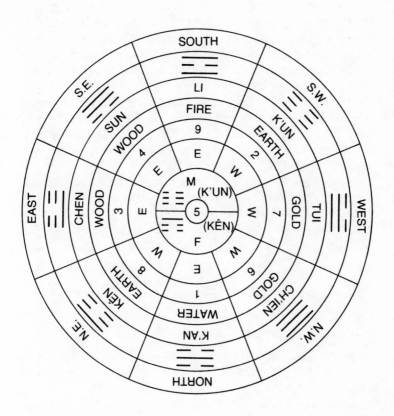

The Pa Che Compass

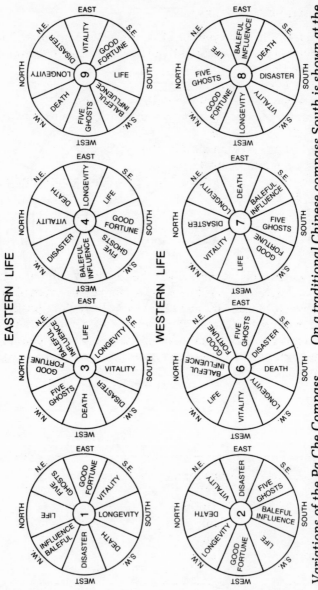

EASTERN LIFE

WESTERN LIFE

Variations of the Pa Che Compass   On a traditional Chinese compass South is shown at the top, but because this book will be used primarily by a western audience the compass points have been reoriented according to normal western usage.

CALCULATIONS FOR WOMEN

Subtract 4 from your year of birth and divide by nine. The remainder is your number. If there is no remainder you must take the number 9.

Example: For a woman born in 1960

$60 - 4 = 56$ divided by $9 = 6$ with a remainder of 2.

The correct reading is found in the compass surrounding number 2.

Example: For a woman born in 1949

$49 - 4 = 45$ divided by $9 = 5$.

The correct reading is found in the compass surrounding number 9.

Not only does the compass gives the reading for the trigram associated with your life, but each segment or direction of the compass represents a trigram. There are always four positive directions and four negative directions that apply to each individual. These different readings can help to explain the varying fortunes of a group of people who live and work in the same place.

Unfavourable directions for a western life

Aspect	Trigram	Element
north	k'an	water
east	chen	wood
south-east	sun	wood
south	li	fire

Unfavourable directions for an eastern life

Aspect	Trigram	Element
south-west	k'un	earth
north-east	ken	earth
west	tui	gold
north-west	ch'ien	gold

Once you have determined the number of your compass, its associated elements, trigram directions and influences, it is also possible to learn which elements and their corresponding colours work in harmony with your life and which bring misfortune. There is also a guide to help you determine auspicious and inauspicious directions, particularly when you are choosing a house.

HARMONIOUS AND DESTRUCTIVE ELEMENTS AND THEIR ASSOCIATED COLOURS

Wood (green) is in harmony with fire (red)
Fire (red) is in harmony with earth (yellow)
Earth (yellow) is in harmony with gold (white)
Gold (white) is in harmony with water (black)
Water (black) is in harmony with wood (green)

Wood (green) destroys earth (yellow)
Earth (yellow) destroys water (black)
Water (black) destroys fire (red)
Fire (red) destroys gold (white)
Gold (white) destroys wood (green)

Once you have found a house suitable for your feng shui reading, make sure that the position of the front door does not weaken your reading. You can check that the position of the house and the position of the front door are aligned by using your appropriate model of the Pa Che feng shui compass created above. Stand at the centre of the house and hold the north point of the compass to the direction of the North Pole. If your feng shui falls into the eastern life group, the main door of your house should be at the north, east, south-east or south. If your feng shui falls into the western life group the main door of your house should be at the west, north-west, south-west or north-east.

5 · MOUNTAINS, TREES AND RIVERS

MOUNTAINS

Mountains and other raised features of the land are yang, and they are not only full of secret cosmological meaning to the geomancer, but are also the protectors of the site. An ideal site is on a slope, open to the south and protected from evil influences by mountains at the north. A pinnacle or a point on the top of the mountain range or a fast running stream on its slopes or at its base will allow the ch'i to be dispersed too rapidly by wind or water.

Steeply flowing waterfalls threaten the site and steep mountain peaks will provide an excess of yang whereas a site that is low-lying among small hills or pools is undesirable since it is a source of excess yin and a likely place for sha to accumulate. A high mountain range as a back drop is acceptable for the site if there are foothills in front so the excess yang caused by towering peaks is lessened.

A headland jutting out from a horse-shoe shaped mountain is a good choice of site as is a peninsula or headland jutting out from the centre of a forking formation. This type of headland is sometimes referred to as the dragon's head. Two gently flowing streams should have their confluence in front of the site and then flow away to the sides, preferably out of sight. On a well-chosen site, these streams or a pool of water with adequate drainage, would be on a flat piece of land known as a Court Altar or Table.

TREES

In the absence of mountains, trees can have the same protective role provided that they are at the back and to the side of the house and not situated at the front. Well-established verdant trees, preferably evergreen, are likely to bring good fortune and are a source of yang. The tree should not be cut or scarred since this will detract from its beneficial influence. Often one well-sited evergreen tree is more important than a grove of trees at the site and is sometimes referred to as a feng shui tree.

WATER

Great attention is paid to the courses of streams and rivers in feng shui since they are one of the natural features of the landscape that is most easily identified and occur on both high and low land. The twists, bends and branches of a river are known as the Water Dragon as opposed to the Mountain Dragon. The various formations of a watercourse are given a feng shui interpretation in the Water Dragon Classic which is found in the Imperial Encyclopedia.

The confluence of two rivers is a positive thing, since influences are concentrated, but a branch in a river often indicates a dispersal of positive forces. A sharp bend in a river is unlucky, since it forms straight, arrowlike lines compared to a meandering river which is considered a natural route of good influence.

The directional flow of rivers and streams is interpreted through the eight trigrams and their influence. The following table indicates the fortune that can result from sharp bends or branches at various compass points:

Sharp bend at

N	children will be thieves, a rich family will become poor
NE	nothing will be left for posterity, childless widows
ENE	disease
E	generations to come will be poor and homeless
ESE	disobedience

Branching at

NE, NW, SE, or SW – prosperity

ENE, WSW, SSE or NNE – poverty, and dispersal of older sons and brothers

E by W, W by S, S by E, N by W – happiness for children

N by E and due W – unhappiness for children

THE WATER DRAGON CLASSIC

> 'If water pours (away from the site) it drains off, it is hurried.
> How can it be abundant and wealth accumulate? If it comes
> in straight and goes out straight it injures men (Secret Arrow).
> Darting left, the eldest son must meet with misfortune; darting
> right, the youngest meet with calamity.'

In the Water Dragon Classic, an ideal site should nestle
among watercourses so it is protected in the stomach of the
dragon. Ch'i flows through watercourses and the branches
that immediately surround a site and protect it are called
inner ch'i, whereas the main trunk of the river that surrounds
the site at the outermost point carries the outer ch'i which is
capable of nourishing the inner ch'i which in turn penetrates
gently into the house or grave. These general classifications
are further defined by the shape of trunks and branches, by
the sharpness of their bends, and by the arrangement of their
shapes.

The illustrations on pages 73 and 74 assess favourable and
unfavourable sites.

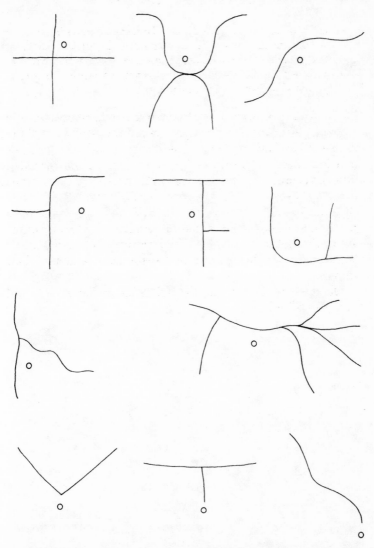

Unfavourable positions for a house. The dot represents the house, the surrounding lines are watercourses.

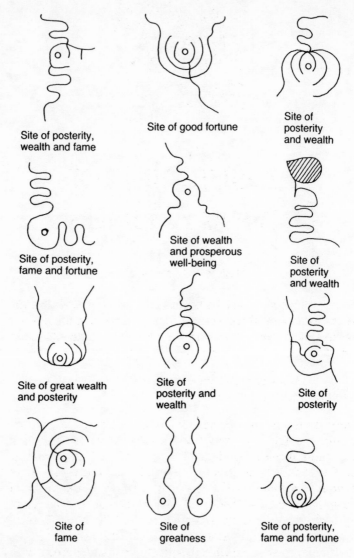

Site of posterity, wealth and fame

Site of good fortune

Site of posterity and wealth

Site of posterity, fame and fortune

Site of wealth and prosperous well-being

Site of posterity and wealth

Site of great wealth and posterity

Site of posterity and wealth

Site of posterity

Site of fame

Site of greatness

Site of posterity, fame and fortune

Favourable positions for a house. The dot represents the house, the surrounding lines are watercourses.

6 · BUILDING OR BUYING A HOUSE

When you plan to buy or build a house, first examine the site of the house, the surrounding buildings and the natural features of the land. According to the fifth century Chinese text, *The Yellow Emperor's Dwelling Classic*

> A good earth will grow exuberant sprouts, a house with good fortune will bring prosperity.

Every house is surrounded by four animal spirits whose position is fixed around the front door of the house. If you stand at the main door of your house facing outwards, the Green Dragon is at your left-hand side, the White Tiger at your right-hand side, the Red Bird is at the front of the house and the Black Tortoise at the back. The Tiger represents mammals, the Dragon represents fish, the Tortoise represents invertebrates, and the Red Bird represents birds. Their colours are also linked with the elements: green with wood, white with gold, red with fire, black with water and the house at the centre is the earth.

In addition to symbolising the animal kingdom and the elements, these semi-mythical creatures also represent the four quarters of the sky: north, south, east and west and in their turn are linked with the four seasons winter, summer, spring and autumn respectively. As well as standing on four sides of a site, the four animals are identified by topographical forms and in particular through the courses of rivers or streams.

The Dragon is seen in a watercourse which has one bend or branch off from the main course. A site situated in this bend can bring wealth, honour and happiness.

The Tiger is seen in a river course with two of three branches. A site positioned in these branches, embraced by the Tiger's water, promises wealth and good fortune for future generations.

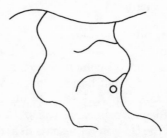

The Tiger is dangerous when two parallel streams turn and branch out. A site located in between their two divergent courses is likened to a tiger holding a corpse in his mouth and heralds poverty and childless old age.

The Red Bird is seen in water-courses which have three back turns. Sites positioned in these turns will be troubled by hunger and poverty. It is believed that men living here will be thieves and women will be coarse.

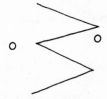

The Tortoise is recognised by the loop resulting from the division of the main water course. This forecasts office and domestic happiness.

BUILDING OR BUYING A HOUSE

The Yang-chai Shih Shu or the Ten Writings on Yang Dwellings describes the conditions needed for an ideal living site:

> All dwellings are very honourable which have on the left flowing water which is the Azure Dragon, on the right a long path, which is the White Tiger, in the front a pool, which is the Red Bird, and behind hills, which are the Sombre Warrior.[1]

The Green Dragon and the White Tiger to the left and right of the house can be likened to guards which must co-ordinate with one another. You should always make sure that there is an even balance between the left and right-hand side of the house. For example, an extension built on the right-hand side of the house, extending into the front garden could herald disaster, since the White Tiger is too powerful for the Dragon to control. It is believed that the White Tiger will emerge to harm those in the house. When the animal spirits are in balance it follows that the forces of yin and yang and the elements are in balance.

On an ideal site, the front of the house is at a lower level than the rear of the house, the Red Bird is lower than the Black Tortoise. A garden that slopes upwards from the front door or steps that lead up from the front door could cause financial and domestic problems. High land at the back of a house protects the house and also provides you with support from family and friends. A back garden that is larger than the front is also interpreted as a support and protector but if the front garden is larger you are likely to miss good opportunities that come your way and in times of trouble you are unlikely to find help from your friends.

The majority of Chinese Buddhist temples and shrines are built on a flat piece of land, square in shape and the same rule should be applied to houses. If the house was originally built on a square plot but a corner of the land has collapsed, been eroded or later used for other construction there could be illness or misfortune in the family. These are the possible problems that could result from damage in one or more directions of your land.

East – could adversely affect the health of the eldest son and bring him misfortune.

South-east – could have a detrimental effect on women in labour and will generally bring bad luck to all women who live in this house.

North-east – could bring illness to the youngest son or grandson.

South-west – the mother or eldest woman will be prone to stomach upset.

North-west – the father or eldest male will be prone to lung disease or high blood pressure.

West – the youngest girl is likely to suffer from poor health.

South – the second daughter will be prone to brain disease and the daughters-in-law will encounter general misfortune.

North – there will be general health problems in the family and the second son will be prone to accidents.

If the front garden of the house is narrower than the back garden the family will enjoy prosperity and praise and there will be unexpected opportunities to further a business since the energy is focused in the area that supports the house. If a house is built on a triangular plot so that the front of the house faces the point of the triangle, everyone living in the house is likely to suffer from ill health, but if the the position of the house is reversed there is a forecast of fatal illness or suicide. Anyone buying a triangular plot of land is advised to buy additional land or to sell part of their land, in order to soften the triangular edge.

For practical health and structural reasons you are advised against buying property that has been built on reclaimed wetlands or dumping sites. Try to choose a house built close to others and in a regular pattern so that the ch'i can move smoothly from building to building. Ch'i has difficulty

Illness and even death could result from living in a house built on a triangular plot.

A fishpond outside the main entrance will bring good fortune and a possible lucky windfall.

passing through scattered houses and irregular planning.

A house should always be at the same height or higher than those directly opposite and slightly lower than those behind so that ch'i can circulate, the houses behind can protect, and pressure from taller buildings to the front can be avoided. A half-moon shaped pond or pool to the front of the main door will encourage wealth, an unexpected windfall and general good fortune. Prosperity and respect are forecast if the rear of the house is square and the front round, for example, bay windows on either side. Try to choose a property with a greater depth than width to encourage happiness and stability in the home. If the house's width is greater than its depth the residents may suffer from mental illness or breathing difficulties.

With the exception of swimming pools, avoid building or buying a house with a pond or pool in the back garden since there will be an excess of yin spirits. If you do have a pond, you can help to establish the balance of yin and yang by planting osmanthus, magnolia or mechilia and avoid planting azaleas or banyan trees. Finally, avoid houses with inner courtyards since this is known as a 'Heaven Well' and the yin spirit is too strong. This area should be used to build living or sleeping accommodation.

7 · Feng Shui in the Home

The Main Door

One of the most important features to take into account when buying a house is the position of the main door. The main door is subject to more traffic than any other part of the house, it is the door that protects the house, and is the means by which destructive spirits can enter the house and one of the ways lucky stars can spread their influence. In general, it is believed that a well-placed front door will encourage health, wealth and long life.

The main door should always be well-hinged, upright and in scale with the size of the house. If the main door is unusually large, it is said to cause a dent in the house and the residents are likely to encounter financial difficulties. If the main door is comparatively small, the residents will be prone to petty arguments.

The door frames are regarded as the supporting poles of the family and should be straight and free of rot. If the frame is bent or weak, the family's fortunes will suffer. It is also advisable to place two lamps outside the front door but if one of the bulbs fails it is considered a bad omen, so remember to replace it immediately. Lamp-posts standing in the garden are regarded as guards of the house and, again, if the bulb of the post is damaged remember to replace it immediately. You should, however, avoid placing a lamp-post directly outside the main door since this could cause financial loss.

Avoid planting trees directly in front of the main door since the strong yin nature of the tree not only blocks the yang entering the house but also sends additional yin inside.

The main door should not face the corner of another house since this corner is likened to a dagger stabbing the main entrance to your home. It will encourage ill health and financial loss. The main door should never face a 'dead end' since the ch'i is unable to circulate, and like still water the energy will stagnate and sha accumulate. Family life is likely to slowly degenerate into petty squabbles arising from

A tree in front of the main entrance brings misfortune because the yin spirit is too strong.

continually walking into the malign forces surrounding the houses. From a practical point of view, a dead end can also make escape difficult in case of fire.

If you are building a house you should place the main door towards the left-hand side, the Green Dragon side, so the dragon can exert his energetic spirit over the house. It is acceptable to place the main door in the centre, but unless your horoscope dictates the direction of the White Tiger you should avoid the right-hand side of the house.

Before buying a house, ensure that the neighbouring building on the right-hand side is not taller or larger than the house you are looking at. Although this is good feng shui for the neighbouring house, it is bad feng shui for you. The spirit of the White Tiger at the right-hand side will outweigh the spirit of the Green Dragon on the left who does not have the power to control the tiger.

The main door should never face directly onto a 'Y' shaped road or path since each time you leave the house you are faced with a choice of direction which will eventually cause misfortune in the family or at work. The main door should never face directly onto churches, temples, monasteries or cemeteries. All these places are full of yin spirits and it is believed that they are the refuge for homeless ghosts, souls and unknown spirits. It is, however, acceptable to buy a house with side or back walls facing religious buildings or cemeteries.

Beware of a main door that faces a narrow gap between two buildings which is likened in feng shui to a slice that has been cut out of a cake. It could cause the family's savings to be slowly frittered away. If you plan to build walls or fences around the house, this will create a beneficial feng shui to protect the house as long as the fences are not too close to the house itself. The protective power of the feng shui is lost if the walls are less than two metres from the house.

A main door facing a mountain or a hill could result in work difficulties or business loss, but you should also avoid buying a house built on a steep hillside and facing a deep

Higher land behind the house protects it and an open aspect to the front encourages prosperity.

valley since this could bring about mental illness. The feng shui of a house located in a bend caused by a stream, river or flyover will encourage ill health and accidents in the family. The watercourse or road is likened to a blade stabbing the house. From a practical point of view, it is believed that the damp air blowing in from the water will cause arthritis or influenza.

CORRECTING BAD FENG SHUI

If you do have a house that has bad feng shui, it is possible to place mirrors at strategic points to divert the malign influences. If, for example, there is a tree directly facing your front door, you are advised to place a feng shui mirror surrounded by the eight trigrams above the door frame so that the bad feng shui is deflected. If you need a second feng shui mirror, choose one without the eight trigrams and with small indentations on the surface of the mirror. If the mirrors are needed in the same place, position the indented mirror on top of the trigram mirror and fix both to the wall above the frame of the door. These mirrors cannot, however, deflect the feng shui caused by a house facing a fork in the road, a dead end or a valley.

THE SITTING-ROOM

The master bedroom, kitchen and sitting-room are the three most important sites for positive feng shui in the house. Since the sitting-room is the area where family and friends gather, it is best situated on the ground floor, within easy access of the main door. It is, however, bad feng shui to have a straight view of a large sitting-room from the main door and, if this happens, and you should try to position a piece of furniture in an appropriate place so part of this view is obscured. This rule does not, however, apply to a small sitting-room. Here you should attempt to create more space by hanging a mirror, but be careful that the bottom steps of the staircase are not reflected in the mirror.

When you are positioning furniture do not place a sofa directly under a beam that can be seen since this will put pressure on whoever is supporting the family. If there is no other place for the furniture, you are advised to have a false ceiling put in to hide the beam. Avoid a cluttered sitting-room since this blocks the flow of the ch'i. It is far better to have paintings or ornaments hanging on the walls than have them gathered on tables or on the floor. An aquarium containing goldfish will also help to increase the flow of ch'i in your house.

The most important point in the sitting-room is known as the wealth point and it is situated on the top left-hand corner as you enter the room. It is believed that a door or a doorway beneath this point will encourage your money to seep away. A kettle or a coffee-maker will also encourage your money to evaporate. If you are suffering from financial problems you are advised to grow a plant with large rounded green leaves there and the growth of the plant will reflect the upturn in your income. The larger the plant and plant pot, the greater the fortune. Avoid growing azaleas or other plants with sharp pointed leaves. It is advisable to place three coins wrapped in red paper under the pot and any dying leaves should be cut away immediately since this is a bad omen. An artificial plant can improve the feng shui in this corner but only a fresh plant can provide the energy and power to attract positive forces.

THE BEDROOM

Since almost a third of our time is spent in bed the feng shui of the bedroom, particularly the master bedroom, is very important. The position of the bed can have an effect on health, prosperity and marriage. You can take a general feng shui reading on the position of your bedroom and bed if you stand at the centre of your house and use the Pa Che compass. However, the more attention that you pay to the positioning of furniture in your bedroom, the greater your fortune.

The base of the bed should be on wheels, never in contact with the floor since this will prevent air from circulating and eventually cause damp in the bed and resulting backaches. Do not store articles under the bed since this will also bring about ill-health. Never set the head of the bed towards the west unless you are advised to do so in your horoscope. This is logical advice in the East since the western side of the house is always the hottest side.

Never set the head of the bed behind the bedroom door, that is when the bedroom door is open only the foot of the bed can be seen because this will result in restless nights. The bed should never be directly opposite the door since this will drain away your energy. If a bed is positioned too close to the window thunder storms will cause restlessness, wet weather may encourage damp and in the long term this positioning may cause liver damage. The bed should never be placed directly under a beam that is visible since this will provoke headaches, mental disorders and loss of creative energy. A beam that crosses over the width of the bed, that is over your stomach as you are lying down, will cause digestion problems. If it crosses over your legs and feet, it will cause swelling in your lower body and problems in your career. To avoid accidents, the bed should never be more than three feet off the ground. Never position a bed directly opposite a mirror since this could not only frighten you should you awake suddenly but may lead to nervous disorders.

If the bedroom is big enough it is easy to follow the rules above but if the bedroom is small it is advisable to follow the traditional Chinese system for setting a bed so that yin and yang are correctly balanced. If you were born in the summer the head of the bed should face north to the cool spirits; if you were born in the winter the bed should face south to the warm spirits. If you were born in the spring or autumn months use the Pa Che system to determine a favourable direction.

Bedside lamps should not be fitted onto the wall directly above the head, if they are, then a lower watt bulb should be used. Very bright overhead bulbs may not only damage eyesight, it is believed they could eventually cause liver disease. A bulb that has blown should be quickly replaced as this is a bad omen for the future. Avoid leaving hand mirrors or make-up sets on a dressing-table directly opposite the foot of the bed since this could have the same effect as a wall mirror in this position. Do not position a dressing-table directly opposite a door since this causes bad temper and emotional problems and a dressing-table that is positioned directly under a beam will create a feeling of general ill-health.

The bedroom door should never face directly onto a kitchen or lavatory door since the steam and other vapours will not only cause sickness but could have a detrimental effect on the family's fortunes.

Decorate your room with colours that correspond to your elements in the Pa Che system. It is advisable to paper or paint the walls in light colours but if you do prefer strong, dark colours then choose patterns that have a light background.

THE KITCHEN

A good feng shui reading for the position of the kitchen and the cooker will encourage good health, family prosperity and harmony. The most favourable positions for the kitchen or cooker are at the southern or eastern side of the house. The element of fire is linked with the south and the element of wood with the east. These are the directions chosen for an eating area since wood is traditionally needed to produce fire to cook food.

In ancient China the majority of stoves were built on the eastern side of the house, and since the majority of the houses faced south it would have been unlucky feng shui to have the cooking area directly opposite the main door. Since wood and charcoal were the two main sources of fuel the south-easterly winds that blew across China were useful for igniting fuel. These were also the two coolest directions and therefore the most suitable places to store food.

The kitchen should be square or rectangular, never triangular. To avoid strong smells or steam entering other rooms the kitchen door should never face directly onto other rooms.

The kitchen is regarded as a 'treasure,' so if the doors at the front or back of the house face the kitchen door the good fortune can easily seep out of the house. A kitchen door that faces a living-room will encourage bad health and arguments and a kitchen that faces a bathroom and lavatory will encourage the spread of germs. You should also check that the plumbing from the lavatory does not run under the kitchen floor.

The cooker should not be set next to a washing basin or close to the sink. If the cooker is next to the sink or refrigerator the elements of fire and water will clash. If the cooker is next to the window, wind can extinguish the gas or sun spoil the food.

It is traditional in many Chinese homes to have a small shrine to the kitchen god set close to the cooker. It is believed that he guards the kitchen listening to the arguments, looking out for good deeds and making a note of mistakes. On the 23rd day of the twelfth month he travels to heaven to offer his annual report to the Jade Emperor, the ruler of heaven. Before setting fire to his portrait so he can fly to heaven, the family smear his lips with honey and burn joss-sticks to ensure a favourable report.

THE BATHROOM AND LAVATORY

The bathroom and lavatory can be built at any side of the house but never in the centre since the odours will spread throughout the house. Do not build a bathroom close to the main door of the house since the excess of yin spirits will clash with the yang spirits coming through the main door.

SHRINES IN THE HOME

If there is adequate space, Chinese and Buddhist families will choose a room close to the centre of the house to build a shrine. If the space is limited, the family will usually place statues and offerings on a shelf in a quiet, clean corner of the house. There should always be an odd number of statues placed in hierarchical order. The Buddha should be at the centre with bodhisattvas standing on either side. Kwan Ti, the god of wealth should be placed to the right of the bodhissatvas and a photograph of the ancestors should be placed to their left. If there is only one statue, for example, Kuan Yin, goddess of mercy, it should be placed in the centre. The shrine should be fixed on an auspicious day chosen from the T'ung Shu, the yearly almanac. The height of the shelf or table on which the statues are placed is measured with a feng shui ruler. Finally, the shelf or the table must not face the lavatory or kitchen door, or be placed under exposed beams.

8 · FENG SHUI AND BUSINESS

The Chinese art of feng shui can be used successfully by those in business to ensure profits and to create a sound business environment. A professional geomancer would say that the quality and pricing of the goods and the reputation of the district can only partially compensate for a site or shop interior that has a bad feng shui.

Many of the feng shui priciples used in the home can also apply to the place of work although there are several additional features to take into account.

THE SITE FOR A SHOP

Choose an area with a dense population, even if there are many other shops in the area. Look for premises built on higher ground to avoid flooding in heavy rains and do not build or choose a shop at a lower level than the neighbouring buildings since the good fortune will drain away. Make sure that the paving or garden area in front of the premises is smooth, clean and well-tended since awkward access will deter customers. The level of the shop floor should also be higher than the level of the road.

THE SHOP INTERIOR

The main entrance of the shop should be wider and higher than domestic premises. Since the house is a private place a small entrance helps to encourage a restful atmosphere and the opposite should apply to a shop. It should be spacious and welcoming to avoid a sense of pressure. The design and colour of your front door is one of the major factors in determining your business fortune. It is the feng shui of the door that will attract the casual passer by. The Chinese say that it is the spirit of good fortune coming from the door that attracts customers into the shop, even if, at first glance, there is nothing in the shop that they particularly need.

After entering the main door, pay particular attention to inside doors directly facing you: they should never be larger than the front door since they exert too much control over the positive spirit of the front door. The Green Dragon is the most fortunate side for the main entrance since the active spirit associated with it will attract business. But if the whole of the shop front is given over to an entrance then make sure that access is through the Green Dragon side. Avoid creating access on the White Tiger side since this is traditionally the quiet side. If the spirit of the White Tiger is disturbed, he will symbolically react by devouring those who enter. In practical terms, this will herald accident or disaster.

The main door should never face the corner of another house or apartment building. This corner represents a dagger ready to stab the access into the shop and this is one of the strict feng shui rules that applies to business or domestic premises. At home this position would cause accident or sickness and at work it will result in long term profit loss. If this positioning is unavoidable the danger can be averted by fixing a screen inside or outside the door so entrance to the building is moved slightly to the side and the bad fortune is blocked.

The main door should never open directly inwards towards a staircase since it will force the wealthy spirit out into the street. This stems from the belief that the staircase is the route that ch'i takes to circulate the house and it could easily be misdirected through an open door into the road.

The main door should not open towards the direction of a lavatory since the yin spirit of this room will rush headlong into the incoming yang spirit from the main door. This sudden clash of opposite spirits is likely to cause illness and misfortune. If the business premises have a kitchen or cooking facilities these must never be seen by someone entering the shop since this could be the cause of fire. This rule does not apply to restaurants or cafes since cooking is at the centre of the business.

The main door should not face temples or churches since the Chinese believe that homeless ghosts and yin spirits dwell in these buildings. These restless spirits will not, however, disturb premises which sell religious statues or artifacts.

As with domestic accommodation, the main door must not face a mountain and the back of the premises should never face a valley or the sea. To avoid debt, make sure that the main door does not face a fork in the road and a main door facing a stream or a river will cause personal sickness as well as a loss in profits.

The main door should not face an outer bend in a fly-over or bridge. The angle of the road can be likened to a sickle cutting into your profits. If, however, the shop faces towards an inner bend, this is likened to your premises being wrapped in a jade belt and, therefore, promises great wealth. It is important never to choose a shop that has an entrance facing the bottom end of a cul-de-sac since there is no escape for the malign spirits that become trapped in the road.

Always keep the main entrance and the area in front of it clean and you should also ensure there are no exposed drain

95

pipes since this will not only block the path of the wealthy spirits as they try to enter the house but it will also drain the good fortune. The best place for drain pipes is at the back of the premises so rainwater is channelled away from the front of the shop. The Chinese say that drains at the front of the house will also cause your capital to drain away.

FENG SHUI IN THE OFFICE

The feng shui of a business is largely determined by the position of the account's office or cash register and the manager's office. The accounts should be reckoned on the White Tiger side of the office; since money is yin in nature it should be matched to the quiet nature of the tiger. The money should be kept in a quiet, concealed and safe place away from windows or doors or mirrors.

It is advisable not to have living accommodation and office space in the same building but if this is unavoidable you should make sure that there are separate lavatories for the two areas. If the accommodation is above the shop, the first-floor lavatory should never be positioned above the manager's room, the accounts office, the cash till or any statues or photographs that you respect. This is done in order to avoid accidents or illness at work. If you run a cafe or restaurant, the cooking area should always face south or east.

The desk is the most important item of furniture in the manager's room. Unless your business is reliant upon visits from clients, the desk should always be in a quiet place away from the public eye. It should be placed against a wall which is likened to a strong mountain offering support and protection. The manager's back should never face windows or doors since the force of the ch'i is too great. This is known in feng shui as the 'empty door' and implies lack of support, concentration and power. The height of the desk should correspond to the 'wealth' and 'prosperity' markings on the feng shui ruler. The desk should never be placed under an exposed beam since this exerts too much pressure nor should it be set at an oblique angle to the shape of the room itself. This would only encourage financial setbacks and staff disagreements. If this does not clash with the directions of your horoscope, a desk placed in one of the corners opposite the door will encourage healthy profits. Other desks in the office should be placed in regular rows around this desk to allow for free movement.

If your feng shui life corresponds to Li or Chen, represented by the elements of fire and wood, you are advised to keep several large leaved green plants in your office. If your feng shui life corresponds to Ken or K'un you should keep the amount of greenery to a minimum, since wood is capable of destroying earth. Two plants at the office door and one plant at the wealthy point will be sufficient. The plants could be replaced by photographs or paintings.

An office devoted to education is suited to landscape paintings in soft colours. Brightly coloured paintings of water lilies, peonies and other large bloomed flowers (except azaleas), are suitable for an office that deals with trade. Police and military offices need stark and regular designs. Black and white calligraphy is well-suited to this environment. Offices that deal with the media are allowed more freedom with their choice of colour and content, but in all cases it is important not to crowd the walls with too much detail or to fill the room with too many plants.

An aquarium containing goldfish is an effective way of combating malign influences and converting negative spirits to positive spirits. There should always be an odd number of fish and the tank should be placed in one of the unlucky directions of your feng shui life.

The rules that govern houses are mostly the same as those that govern shops or offices. You are, however, warned not to choose a shop or office building that combines several shapes in its groundplan.

APPENDIX

The relationship between the living and the dead is an important and effective part of Chinese family life. By choosing a positive burial site the feng shui expert ensures that the deceased not only rests peacefully but is provided with an appropriate gateway to the next world. But this is only the first phase of the lifelong relationship that the living maintain with their ancestors. The needs of the ancestors are maintained by their relatives and in return for this continued care the spirit of the ancestors bestow good fortune on the living.

This appendix lists the annual festivals that commemorate the dead.

CHING MING

The festival of Ching Ming falls in the spring usually on the 5th or 6th April during the end of the second, or beginning of the third months of the lunar calendar. Ching Ming means 'clear and bright' and is one of the twenty-four phases of the year referred to on page 46. It is a time associated with the resurgence of life in spring and it is traditional for women and children to wear willow catkin to protect themselves at a future time from being reborn as dogs during the transmigration of souls.

The focus of the festival is a visit to the ancestral spirits who hover around the tombs. Cemeteries are often built close to farming land and since this is the beginning of the agricultural year the spirits of the dead can be called upon to help bring a fruitful harvest. When families visit the grave, they first sweep away the debris that has gathered on and around the grave during the previous year and repaint the inscriptions to the dead. Incense sticks and red candles are lit before the inscription and photo of the deceased on the headstone, paper clothes and 'spirit' money are also burnt so the dead are provided with fresh supplies for the afterlife and rice, wine, tea, chicken, fruit and other food is left on the grave. Many of these foods are chosen for their special associations with good fortune and a speciality at Ching Ming is bean curd with fish heads and tails. Fish implies profit and the heads and tails give the offering a sense of wholeness. The word 'fu' from 'tao fu', meaning bean curd, sounds similar to the word 'wu', meaning protect. The wish is that the ancestors, who are hopefully satisfied with the siting of their graves and comforted by their relatives, will protect their descendants.

Since the well-being of the living family is so closely intertwined with that of dead relatives this is a time to renew contact with the dead and the celebratory picnic that is held after the offerings have been made takes place on the hillside close to the grave so the spirits of the dead are present. Before the family leave, they tuck several strips of offering paper under a stone on top of the grave as a sign that the grave has been tended for that year.

This is also the day to visit the ancestral hall, if the family still have one and if it is accessible. The ancestral hall is the building that contains tablets listing the names of the clan's founding ancestor and other deceased members of the family. The founding ancestor's tablet is put in a position of prominence on the main altar and those who were distinguished in life, produced large families or were wealthy, also have positions of prominence on smaller altars to the left and right. The tablets belonging to the most prestigious members of the family are not removed but the tablets of those who were not so highly regarded are shifted to the back of the hall to make room for tablets belonging to the newly deceased. The well-being of the dead, the living and those yet to be born is linked through the existence of these ancestral halls. In as much as the family revolved around the founder of their clan during his life time so it is after his death. These ancestral halls are not only places of rememberance, in the past they have been places of worship, community centres and council chambers, although with the widespread Chinese diaspora many Chinese are unable to visit these halls.

The rituals that are performed here are performed on behalf of the whole clan. Through the offerings and ritual the dead souls maintain their vitality, the living will be guided and protected by their ancestors and those who have yet to be born will have the blessings of their deceased relatives when their names are inscribed in the register of births kept in the ancestral hall. Many families will also have a smaller ancestral shrine in their home and similar offerings are made and prayers said before these shrines at Ching Ming.

THE HUNGRY GHOST FESTIVAL

The fifteenth day of the seventh lunar month is the time to remember the spirits of those who have left this world without a proper burial or who have no relatives to care for them. Ancestors who have relatives are considered 'tso sin' – former holy fathers, but those who are abandoned are 'kwai' – disembodied spirits or ghosts. Unlike the ancestors they are not sustained by paper food and money or by offerings at the shrine, the living do not turn to them for help or advice and they have no place to rest. This lack of respect makes them bitter and they retaliate by creating danger in the world of the living which is why they have to be placated.

The Seventh Moon is a particularly disturbing time for many Chinese since the gates of the underworld are opened to allow these unfortunates to wander in the world of the living. Their anger can be soothed if they are presented with the same offerings that are given to the ancestors and gods. Their anger is further assuaged if they are entertained by several days of opera.

Amongst the Boat People in Hong Kong the celebrations are arranged on a family basis and in Hong Kong they are arranged by elders of the area or by the Residents' Association. House to house collections are made to subsidise this event and the amount received decides the scale of the celebrations which are housed in temporary constructions built around open spaces. A theatre is built at one end and an altar where huge sticks of incense are constantly burnt is constructed at the other end. Deities are carried in sedan chairs from local temples and reside in a temporary temple behind the altar. The organising committee usually organises its office at one side of the shrine and the remaining space is occupied by piles of offerings, Buddhist and Taoist headquarters and a huge paper statue of Tai Si Wong. It is believed that Tai Si Wong, who holds a notebook and pen, records the deeds of those at the festival and makes his report to the Jade Emperor at the end of the festival. Close by there is usually a statue of the boddhisatva, Kuan Yin, the goddess of mercy. Some say that she once held a feast for the Hungry Ghosts but they behaved so badly she was forced to invite the King of Hell to her next party so he could maintain order. From that time on the ghosts have behaved correctly in her company. Others say that although Kuan Yin is a compassionate deity there are times when she has to appear fierce to correct unruly behaviour and so she appears at the Hungry Ghost festival as Tai Si Wong.

In the lead up to the festival in the first two weeks of the seventh moon families make private offerings to the ghosts in a ceremony known as shiu yi, 'burning clothes'. Those who live close to the sea sail out to pray and scatter rice on the waters or launch small paper boats carrying food and paper offerings to appease the ghosts who have been lost at sea.

On the last evening of this festival, usually on the fifteenth day of the seventh moon, the paper 'Bank of Hell' notes, paper clothes, furniture, transport and food are sent to the ghosts. The paper goods are burnt and once the food has been offered so that they are spiritually satisfied it is shared amongst those present. As the festival draws to its close the huge paper statue of Tai Si Wong is carried from one end of the bonfire to the other so he can assess the efforts that have been made and then he, too, is burnt so he can make his report in Heaven.

CH'UNG YEUNG – THE DOUBLE NINTH

During the first nine days of this month the gods lift restrictions on those who abide in the underworld and the living are able to communicate with their dead relatives. On the ninth day many Chinese visit the graves of their ancestors and clear away the decaying growth of the summer. Bank of Hell notes are burnt and paper clothes are offered to protect the dead against the oncoming cold of the winter. Once the family have paid their respects they share a picnic at the grave. This is the second remembrance festival of the year and it varies from family to family whether both days or just one of these days is celebrated. This is also the time for families who live within distance to visit their ancestral hall and to make offerings to their clan ancestor and others whose names are listed there.

NOTES

INTRODUCTION

1. Stephen Feuchtwang, *An Anthropological Analysis of Chinese Geomancy*, Vithagna, Southern Materials Center Inc., Taipei, 1974, 1st edition, p. 15.

1. LIVING IN HARMONY

1. Huai Nan Tzu, quoted in Theodore de Bary (ed.), *Sources of Chinese Tradition*, Columbia University Press, 1960, Vol. I, pp. 192–193.
2. Originally told in J. Eberhard, *Chineses Fairy Tales and Folk Tales*, London, 1937.

2. SYMBOLS OF HEAVEN AND EARTH

1. J. Needham, *Science and Civilisation in China*, Cambridge University Press, 1956, Vol. II, p. 243.
2. Shoo King, *The Great Plan*, (trans.) James Legge, *The Chinese Classics*, OUP, 1871, Vol. III, reprinted by Southern Materials Center Inc., Taipei, 1983.
3. *Ch'uan Commentary*, Book X, Year 25, (trans.) James Legge, op.

cit., Vol. V, p. 708.

4. Chu Hsi, *Collected Works*, (trans.) J. Needham, op. cit., Vol. II, pp. 477–8.

5. B.C. Henry, *The Cross and the Dragon*, New York, 1885, p. 142.

6. BUILDING AND BUYING A HOUSE

1. Yang chai Shih Shu, *Ten Writings on Yang Dwellings* quoted in Stephen Feuchtwang, op. cit., p. 158.

BIBLIOGRAPHY

Baker, Hugh, *More Ancestral Images*, South China Morning Post Publications, 1980, and *Ancestral Images Again*, South China Morning Post Limited, Hong Kong, 1981.

Bary, Theodore de (ed.), *Sources of Chinese Tradition*, Columbia University Press, 1960

Burkhardt, V.R., *Chinese Creeds and Customs*, South China Morning Post Publications, Hong Kong, 1982

Chamberlain, Jonathon, *Chinese Gods*, Long Island Publishers, Hong Kong, 1983

Dore, Henry S.J., *Chinese Customs*, (trans.) by M. Kennelly, S.J., Graham Brash Publishers, Singapore, 1987

Eberhard, J., *Chinese Fairy Tales and Folk Tales*, London, 1937

Feuchtwang, Stephen D.R., *An Anthropological Analysis of Chinese Geomancy*, Southern Materials Center, Inc., Taipei, 1st edition, 1974

Henry, B.C., *The Cross and the Dragon*, New York, 1885

Law, Joan, and Ward, Barbara E., *Chinese Festivals*, South China Morning Post Publications, Hong Kong, 1982

Legge, James, *The Chinese Classics*, Oxford University Press, 1871, Southern Materials Center, Inc., Taipei, 1983, Vols. III and V

Lip, Evelyn, *Chinese Geomancy*, Times Books International, 1979

Man-Ho, Kwok, *Authentic Chinese Horoscopes*, Arrow, London, 1987

Needham, Joseph, *Science and Civilisation in China*, Cambridge University Press, 1956, Vol. II, 1959, Vol. III

O'Brien, Joanne, *Chinese Myths and Legends,* Arrow, London, 1990

Palmer, Martin, Kwok Man-Ho, O'Brien, Joanne, *The Fortune Teller's I Ching,* Century, London, 1986

INDEX